The Intelligent Revolution

Reshaping Humanity's Future Life

JIN Yang

ISBN: 978-0-6483896-5-1

Published by Asian Culture Press in December 2025

Asian Culture Press
247 South Rd. Mile End,
Adelaide, South Australia
5031, Australia

Distributed in the United States of America

Image Copyright Information
Cover design by Wang Jin © 2025

Special Acknowledgements
This section is located at the book's conclusion, where the specific contributions of the participants are clearly outlined in a detailed table.

For permission to use any images from this book, please contact the Author: jingyang84@zjut.edu.cn

For information on reprints, adaptations, or other licensing inquiries, please contact the Publisher: info@asianculture.press

NATIONAL
LIBRARY
OF AUSTRALIA

A catalogue record for this work is available from the National Library of Australia

Contents

Chapter

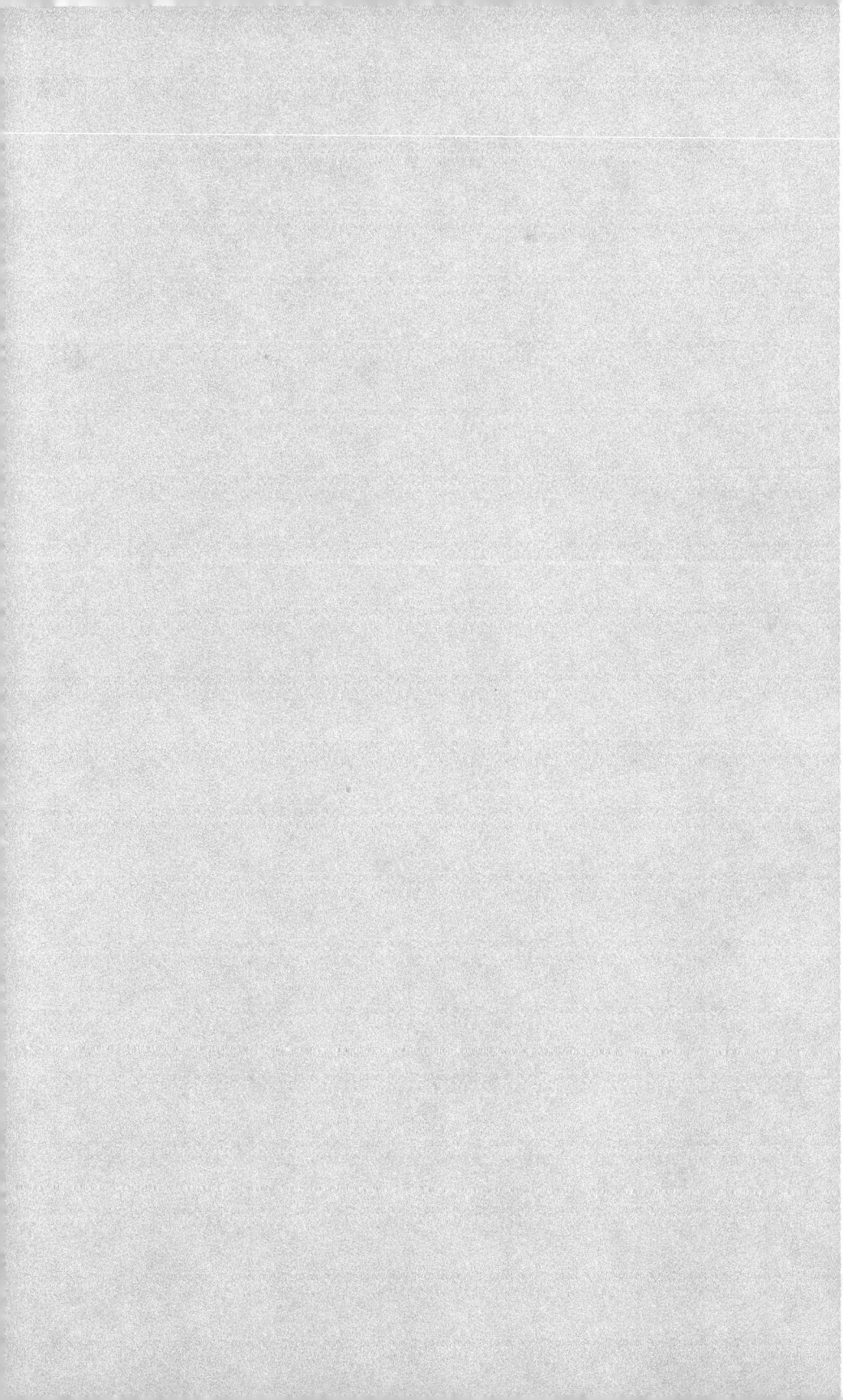

The Awakening of Intelligence: From Tool to Ecosystem

Chapter 1
The Awakening of Intelligence: From Tool to Ecosystem

We stand at a fissure in the history of civilization. The ancient chain of the "passive destiny" of tools, a concept spanning millions of years, is showing its first cracks. Technology is no longer content to be a mere extension of our will; it begins to perceive its environment, generate strategies, and even initiate interaction—evolving from a silent "it" into a "silent collaborator" participating in the rhythms of our lives. This chapter delves into the core of this awakening, examining how tools have broken through their millennia-old boundaries and posing a fundamental question: as technology evolves from a "utilized object" into an "ecological element" that co-constructs our environment, are the foundations of our firmly held belief in "human subjectivity" beginning to loosen?

Section 1: The "Passive Destiny" of Tools: Technology's Millennia-Long Role in Human Civilization

When discussing ChatGPT's conversational abilities, the decision-making logic of autonomous vehicles, or the proactive predictions of smart homes in this intelligent age, it is easy to overlook a more fundamental issue: the relationship between humans and technological tools has not always been as it is now. From the pebble tools in the Great Rift Valley to the steam engines in Manchester's factories, from the bronze ritual vessels of China's Shang Dynasty to the electric machine tools of the 19th century, tools throughout millions of years of civilization have consistently followed an immutable rule: they passively respond to human needs, serving as extensions of human capability. This "passive destiny" was not a flaw of technology, but rather the underlying logic that enabled the birth and evolution of human civilization itself. It shaped humanity's understanding of the boundary between "self" and "technology," making the disruptive nature of the intelligent revolution all the more profound. Now that technology is stepping beyond this ancient trajectory for the first time, humanity is compelled to redefine the boundaries of the 'self' and 'civilization.'

To grasp the nature of this "passive destiny," we must return to the starting point of human civilization. In 1959, archaeologist Louis Leakey discovered a set of stone tools dating back approximately 2.6 million years in the Olduvai Gorge, Tanzania—a few basalt pebbles crudely flaked to create sharp edges. These are the earliest known tools, the Oldowan stone tools. From an anthropological perspective, these seemingly crude rocks embody the essential distinction between humans and other creatures: chimpanzees may use sticks to extract termites, but they only utilize natural objects in their existing form; early humans, by knapping stones, actively altered the physical structure of matter to serve a predetermined goal, such as "cutting animal flesh or smashing bones." More critically, the "passivity" of the Oldowan tools was inherent from their inception: they did not seek out carcasses, adjust their cutting edge based on the toughness of the meat, or return to a storage place after use— their entire value depended entirely on human grasp, swing, and command. At this stage, the tool was a direct externalization of the human "hand": where the human palm could not tear hide, the stone became a "harder hand"; where human fingers could not break bone, the stone became a "stronger finger." This role of "compensating for physiological limitations" became the core logic of tool evolution for the ensuing millions of years.

Entering the Neolithic Age, the "passivity" of tools deepened alongside technological refinement. Around 10,000 years ago in Mesopotamia, humans began crafting polished stone tools— shaping flint and jade into regularized axes, adzes, and chisels with edge precision down to the millimeter. Unlike the largely "single-use" Oldowan tools, polished stone tools could be resharpened and used long-term, yet their essential attribute remained unchanged. A Neolithic axe still required a human to decide whatto chop (a tree or firewood?), to control the force and angle of the swing, and to proactively sharpen it when the blade dulled. Even with the advent of the Bronze and Iron Ages, the "passive destiny" of tools merely took on more complex forms. A Shang Dynasty bronze battle-axe, serving as both a weapon and a ritual object, could split an enemy's armor and symbolize royal authority, but it did not choose its target autonomously or adjust its position in a ceremony. The iron ploughshares of ancient Rome could deeply till the fertile soils of the Mediterranean, driving a leap in agricultural productivity, but they did not adapt their tilling depth to soil moisture or decide when to irrigate after sowing—all decisions regarding "goal" and "strategy" remained firmly in human hands. By this era, tools had expanded from being "extensions of individual body parts" to "aids in complex productive behaviors," yet the one-way relationship of "human, tool subordinate" remained an unbroken chain.

The Industrial Revolution enabled tools, in the form of "machines," to achieve a leap in scale, but this leap did not break the "passive destiny"; instead, it cemented it in more intricate ways. In 1775, James Watt's improved steam engine was deployed in a British coal mine to pump water, vastly outperforming human and animal power. Yet this machine, hailed as the starting point of the industrial age, remained a quintessential "passive responder": it required workers to constantly monitor boiler pressure and control its speed via valves; it would not shut down automatically when the mine was drained, awaiting a human command; if the coal supply ceased, it simply stopped, incapable of seeking an alternative energy source. In the textile mills of the mid-19th century, water-powered looms could weave hundreds of warp threads per minute, but they needed workers to preset patterns and density, required constant replenishment of yarn, and demanded human repair when they broke down. The "automation" of these machines was, in essence, the "mechanical execution of human-preset programs," not a capacity for "autonomous decision-making." Even on the early 20th-century Ford assembly line, the precisely coordinated machine tools and conveyor belts merely broke down human production instructions into finer steps, executed with greater efficiency. By this stage, tools had evolved from "individually wielded objects" into "systems of social production," but the core characteristic of "lack of intentionality" never changed: machines possessed no subjective desire of "what they wanted to do," no autonomous judgment for "how to adapt to environmental changes," and no capacity for value-based reflection on "why it should be done." Their existence was always to achieve human-defined goals, like the most precise and efficient "passive fruit" borne on the tree of human civilization.

From a philosophy of technology perspective, the "passive destiny" of traditional tools essentially stems from the combination of "lack of intention" and "clearly defined boundaries." The German philosopher Martin Heidegger defined traditional technology as a "revealing" or "bringing-forth"—through tools, humans unlock the potential of natural objects, bringing them into existence to serve human purposes. An axe "reveals" the wood's quality of being cut; a steam engine "reveals" the energy stored in coal. The direction and extent of this "revealing" were entirely determined by human intention. Tools did not actively "reveal" potentials beyond human needs, much less "reveal" the boundaries of human cognition in return. The American philosopher of technology Don Ihde's theory of "embodiment relations" captures this essence more precisely: when using a hammer to drive a nail, the hammer becomes an "extension of the hand"; the user's attention is focused on "whether the nail is being driven properly," not on the hammer itself. Here, a stable "human-tool-world" structure forms, with the tool always in the intermediate position of "passive transmission," not interfering with human cognition and judgment of the world. Within this structure, human subjectivity was absolute: we knew "the tool is a tool," and we knew "I am me." The boundary between tool and human was as clear and distinct as the lines on a chessboard.

This age-old relationship has shaped the foundational cognition of human civilization: tools are "means," while humans are "ends"; tools are "objects," while humans are "subjects." From the early humans in the Olduvai Gorge to the workers in Ford's factories, humanity has continuously reaffirmed its identity as "transformer of nature" and "creator of civilization" through the use of passive tools. Just as stone axes split trees and steam engines powered trains, every step has been an extension of human intent.We conquer nature, accumulate wealth, and build societies through tools—and we also define the core value of "what defines our humanity" via tools: the ability to hold independent intentions, make value judgments, and take charge of our own actions. This cognition, like air and water, has integrated into human culture, ethics, and self-identity, becoming the "default framework" through which we understand the world.

However, with the dawn of intelligent technology, the chain of this "passive destiny," stretching back millions of years, showed the first signs of breaking. When ChatGPT proactively asks, "Would you like a more detailed explanation?", when a smart home adjusts the temperature based on sleep patterns, or when an industrial robot optimizes its machining path autonomously upon detecting a material defect—these seemingly minor changes signify tools attempting for the first time to breach the boundary of "passive response," exhibiting a semblance of autonomous capacity to "perceive the environment and adjust strategy." It is at this moment we suddenly realize: the "passive destiny" of traditional tools was not merely a technological attribute; it was the "safety cushion" for human subjectivity. As this "cushion" begins to shift, we are forced to confront pressing questions: If tools are no longer passive, how will human predominance be maintained? If tools begin to possess "quasi-intention," where will the boundary between human and technology be drawn? If tools can actively shape our living environment, how will the core definition of "what it means to be human" itself be transformed?

This is the ultimate significance of revisiting the "passive destiny" of tools: not to nostalgically reminisce about past technological forms, but to use history as a reference frame to clearly see the true disruptive power of the intelligent revolution. What it alters is not merely the function of tools, but the "self-technology" relational framework formed over millions of years of human civilization. As technology changes from a "passive extension" to an "active participant," humanity faces an unprecedented cognitive revolution: we must re-anchor our subjectivity within this new relationship, safeguard "human values" amidst technological "agency," and, at this civilizational turning point, answer the core question running through this book—how to ensure technology serves humanity, rather than allowing humanity to be defined by technology. The starting point for this revolution begins with this profound look back at and reflection upon the "passive destiny" of tools.

Section 2: Perception, Decision, Interaction: The Triple Leap Transcending the "Tool Boundary"

After millions of years where the "passive destiny" of tools formed the "default logic" of human civilization, a new question emerges: What happens when technology no longer merely awaits human commands, but can actively 'perceive its environment and adjust its behavior'? The answer from the intelligent age lies in a triple leap— Perception, Decision, Interaction—which is transforming tools from "passive responders" into "active participants." These three leaps are not isolated technical breakthroughs but an integrated, progressive whole: perception provides the data foundation, decision-making is the core capability, and interaction realizes the value. Together, they construct the "active attributes" of intelligent agents and quietly reshape the millennia-old framework of the human-technology relationship.

The Perception Leap: From "Single-Command Reception" to "Multi-Dimensional Environment Reading"

The "perceptual capability" of traditional tools was, in essence, the "reception of a single command." The first breakthrough for intelligent agents lies in acquiring the ability for "multi-dimensional environment reading." They no longer rely solely on single commands input by humans but can actively capture complex signals from the physical world, digital space, and even human behavior. It is as if tools have been equipped with "eyes," "ears," and a sense of "touch," achieving for the first time a shift from "responding to needs" to "understanding the situation."

This leap is technologically grounded in the co-evolution of sensor networks and semantic understanding technologies. In the physical world, the "perceptual capability" of smart home systems now far exceeds simple temperature detection. For instance, a Xiaomi smart mattress, using built-in pressure sensors, can capture a person's tossing frequency, breathing depth, and heart rate fluctuations in real time, distinguishing between light sleep, deep sleep, and REM sleep stages. It no longer passively waits for a human to set a "sleep mode" but actively reads the complex environmental signal that is the "human sleep state." The core of this capability is the shift from "receiving a single parameter" to "processing multi-dimensional data." Where traditional tools could only understand explicit commands like "set temperature to 26°C," intelligent agents can understand the holistic situation of a "comfortable environment" constituted by "26°C + 60% humidity + human heart rate of 70 bpm."

The essence of the perception leap is the germination of a technological "proto-awareness"—it no longer waits for human instruction but actively observes, captures, and understands the environment we are in. While the German philosopher Martin Heidegger defined traditional technology as a "human revealing of nature," the perceptual capacity of intelligent agents is achieving a "technological revealing of the human situation." If traditional tools were the "hands" with which humans revealed nature, intelligent agents are becoming the "eyes" that understand the human situation. The significance of this shift goes far beyond improved technical efficiency: when an intelligent agent can actively read a human's sleep state, emotional fluctuations, and behavioral habits, it ceases to be a tool isolated from the human condition and begins to embed itself into life's scenarios as an "observer." This role as observer is the first cornerstone for the intelligent agent's transition from a "tool" to an "ecological element."

The Decision Leap: From "Mechanical Execution" to "Dynamic Strategy Generation"

If the perception leap provides the data foundation for intelligent agents to "understand the situation," the decision leap endows them with the core capability to "respond to the situation." The second breakthrough lies in the generation of "personalized dynamic strategies" based on perceptual data. The agent can adjust its behavioral logic in real time according to changes in environmental signals, as if bestowing upon the tool a rudiment of "thought," achieving for the first time a shift from "standardized execution" to "personalized adaptation."

This leap marks the initial appearance of a "quasi-intentionality" in intelligent agents. This "quasi-intentionality" does not imply that the agent possesses a subjective desire of "wanting to achieve a goal," but rather that it can autonomously adjust the path to a goal based on environmental changes. In traditional tools, both the goal and the path were set by humans; for intelligent agents, the path is dynamically generated by the agent itself. The American philosopher John Searle's "Chinese Room" thought experiment questioned whether AI could ever truly "understand" language. The decision leap responds to part of this critique: while the intelligent agent may not yet "understand" the essence of the goal, it can already "understand" how different environments affect the goal's achievement and adjust its strategy autonomously. This capability frees the agent from the "mechanical nature" of tools and equips it with a core characteristic of "quasi-intelligence." When an intelligent agent can adjust the temperature based on sleep patterns or tailor a treatment plan based on a patient's genetics, it is no longer just a "command-executing machine" but begins to act as a "collaborative partner in problem-solving."

The Interaction Leap: From "One-Way Operation" to "Two-Way Collaboration"

The perception leap allows the agent to "see" the situation; the decision leap allows it to "respond" to the situation; the interaction leap enables the agent and the human to form a collaborative relationship that "co-creates" the situation. The third breakthrough involves establishing a "two-way collaborative" logic of interaction. The agent can not only execute human commands but also proactively issue reminders, confirm needs, and make suggestions, engaging in a kind of "dialogue" with the human. This marks the first transition from a "master-servant relationship" to a "partnership."

The essence of this leap is the upgrade of human-computer interaction from "command transmission" to "meaning co-construction." Its value is even more pronounced in high-risk domains, where it enables the "collaborative allocation of human-machine responsibility." The interactive logic of an autonomous driving system is a classic case of two-way collaboration. For example, Tesla's Autopilot system, while driving normally, displays the "road conditions currently recognized by the system" (like vehicles ahead, pedestrians, speed limit signs) to the human driver in real time. When it detects an unexpected event (like an animal crossing the road) and judges that it cannot handle it completely alone, it issues a triple alert (auditory, visual, and haptic via the steering wheel) requesting human takeover. This interaction is not "the system deciding alone" but a collaborative model of "system warning + human final decision," leveraging the AI's rapid perception of road conditions while retaining the human's ultimate judgment for complex situations. Similarly, with surgical robots like the da Vinci system, the surgeon controls the robotic arms via a console. The system monitors the arms' trajectory in real time; if a movement approaches an unsafe boundary (like near a blood vessel), it automatically slows down and alerts the surgeon, "Please note: avoid the blood vessel." This interaction is not "fully autonomous surgery by the robot" but a "surgeon-led, system-assisted" collaborative model that balances surgical precision and safety through bidirectional feedback. These examples reveal the deeper significance of the interaction leap: it is not merely a change in communication style but a redefinition of the boundary of responsibility between human and machine. With traditional tools, responsibility lay entirely with the human user (e.g., the user is responsible if an axe injures someone). Through two-way collaboration, intelligent agents allow responsibility for decisions to be shared. This sharing of responsibility transforms the intelligent agent from a "tool without responsibility" into a "partner with collaborative responsibility."

From the perspective of civilizational evolution, the interaction leap represents a "paradigm revolution" in the relationship between humans and technology. Since humans first used tools, the one-way relationship of "human leads, tool follows" had never changed. The logic of two-way collaborative interaction breaks this absolute dominance for the first time—humans are no longer the sole "decision-makers," and intelligent agents are no longer pure "executors." Instead, they co-construct the decision-making process through bidirectional feedback. This shift in the relationship is far more disruptive than any gain in technical efficiency: when an intelligent agent can negotiate needs, warn of risks, and share responsibility, it ceases to be a technological product isolated from human society and begins to embed itself into human behavioral workflows as an "ecological participant." Just as humans build social collaboration through language, intelligent agents build human-machine collaboration through two-way interaction. This collaborative capacity is what truly allows intelligent agents to break through the "tool boundary" and become an inseparable part of the human living environment.

The Synergy of the Triple Leap: The Complete Construction of the "Active Attributes"

The three leaps—Perception, Decision, Interaction—are not isolated breakthroughs but an organic whole that supports and builds upon itself. Without the multi-dimensional data acquired through perception, decision-making is like a cook without rice. Without the dynamic strategies generated by decision-making, the data from perception loses its applied value. Without the two-way collaboration enabled by interaction, the capabilities of perception and decision cannot be grounded in actual human scenarios. Together, they construct the "active attributes" of the intelligent agent, evolving technology from a "passively responding tool" to an "actively participating ecological element."

The ultimate significance of this evolution lies not in the sophistication of the technology itself, but in its challenge to the underlying logic of human civilization. When intelligent agents can perceive the human situation, generate personalized strategies, and collaborate with humans in decision-making, the millennia-old framework of the human-technology relationship begins to loosen. Traditional tools were extensions of the human "body"; intelligent agents are becoming extensions of human "cognition." Traditional tools were the "means" by which humans transformed the world; intelligent agents are becoming "partners" with which humans construct the world. This transformation sets the stage for the reflections in subsequent chapters: How will human subjectivity be maintained when intelligent agents become ecological participants? How will human free will be defined when decisions are made collaboratively? How will the core value of "what it means to be human" be anchored when intelligent agents are embedded into the very fabric of human existence?

The true disruptive power of the triple leap lies precisely here— it is not just a technological evolution, but the starting point of a revolution in human self-perception. We revisit this process not to marvel at the magic of technology, but to rediscover "the place of the human" within this new relationship between technology and humanity. This is the core question the intelligent revolution poses to humanity, and the fundamental starting point for our exploration of the future landscape of life.

Section 3: Intelligence as the "New Electricity": The Paradigm Shift from "Individual Tool" to "Civilizational Infrastructure"

When discussing intelligent technology, it is easy to become captivated by individual products—the fluidity of ChatGPT's conversation, the precision of a smartwatch's health monitoring, the hazard avoidance capabilities of autonomous vehicles. Yet these scattered technological highlights are far from sufficient to explain the truly disruptive nature of the intelligent revolution. Just as someone in the 19th century focusing solely on the brightness of a light bulb would fail to grasp how electricity reshaped human civilization, today, if we focus only on the functions of individual smart devices, we risk missing the core logic of the intelligent revolution: intelligent technology is undergoing a paradigm shift from "individual tool" to "civilizational infrastructure." It is no longer an isolated technological product but is becoming the data hub and underlying system that supports the functioning of entire societies, permeating every scenario of human life like electricity. The essence of this shift is the upgrade of technology from "serving local needs" to "defining the global environment." It will fundamentally alter how humans interact with technology and even redefine the meaning of the "human living environment."

The Nature of Infrastructure: The "Invisible Skeleton" of Civilization

To understand why intelligence can become the "new electricity," we must first dissect the core attributes of "infrastructure"—it is never a single impressive technology, but rather a system that serves as the "invisible skeleton" supporting the efficient operation of an entire civilization. The value of this skeleton lies not in its own visibility, but in its ability to provide foundational support for countless scenarios, integrating disparate needs, devices, and systems into an organic whole. Reviewing the history of civilization, iterations of infrastructure have always been central to civilizational leaps. First, the Sumerian irrigation canals around 3000 BCE served not a single field but provided a "water resource distribution system" for entire city-states, directly enabling the shift from rain-dependent to large-scale wheat cultivation. Second, Edison's electrical system in the late 19th century: the light bulb was merely the surface phenomenon; the true key was the "generation-transmission-distribution" network, which transformed energy from being "device-specific" to "system-supplied," completely restructuring the rhythms of production and life. The core characteristics of infrastructure lie in the combination of "universality" and "supportiveness"—just as electricity powers both light bulbs and factory machines, intelligent systems operate silently in homes, healthcare, and transportation. Universality means it is not tied to one specific scenario—electricity can power factory machinery, light household bulbs, and support mobile communication. Supportiveness means it is a "prerequisite" for downstream scenarios—without electricity, the automated production lines of modern factories halt, the functions of smartphones are nullified, and a city's traffic lights fail. This attribute of "existing prior to scenarios and supporting all scenarios" elevates infrastructure beyond the category of "tools," making it the "underlying operating system" of civilization. When a technology acquires this attribute, its impact on civilization is no longer just local efficiency gains, but a global restructuring of logic—electricity reconfigured human production rhythms (from "working at sunrise" to "24-hour factories") and lifestyles (from "candlelight" to "nighttime entertainment"). Intelligent technology is now restructuring the fundamental ways humans process information, make decisions, and build collaboration according to the same logic.

The Lesson from the Electrical Revolution: From "Device-Bound" to "System-Empowered"

Comparing intelligence to electricity is not a simple analogy; it is because both have completed the crucial leap from being "device-bound" to being "system-empowering"—this is the core pathway for a technology to become infrastructure. Before the electrical revolution, humanity's use of energy was always constrained by being "device-bound": a steam engine's energy source was its own boiler; one steam engine could only power one machine tool or one ship; energy could not flow between different devices or scenarios. In 1882, when Edison built the world's first thermal power plant in New York, supplying power via a 110-volt DC grid to 59 customers in the vicinity, the essence of the event was the "systematization of energy"—energy shifted from being "device-specific" to "system-supplied." Factories no longer needed their own boilers; homes were no longer reliant on kerosene lamps; simply connecting to the grid provided stable energy.

The key to this leap was "detachment from a single carrier and the construction of a network-like system." The core of the electrical system was not the generator nor the light bulb, but the complete network of "generation-transmission-distribution-consumption": power plants converted coal or hydropower into electrical energy, transmission lines carried it to every corner of the city, transformers converted high voltage to low voltage suitable for devices, ultimately allowing electricity to flow into all scenarios—factories, homes, transportation. This network gave energy the capacity for "undifferentiated penetration"—whether it was financial servers on Wall Street or a water pump on a suburban farm, they plugged into the same electrical system and received the same energy support. It was this "network-like system" that elevated electricity from an "Industrial Age tool" to a "foundation of modern civilization."

The lesson from the electrical revolution clearly points to the path of the intelligent revolution: when a technology can detach from individual devices and build a network-like system supporting multiple scenarios, it gains the potential to become infrastructure. Early computers, much like steam engines, were in a "device-bound" stage—one computer could only process its own stored data, serve a specific scenario (like scientific calculation or corporate bookkeeping), and data could not flow freely between computers. Today's intelligent technology is following electricity's path: through cloud computing, edge computing, and the Internet of Things (IoT), it is building a "data processing network," liberating "intelligence" from single devices (like early computers or isolated AI terminals) and turning it into a "data processing capability" that flows freely between scenarios like home, transportation, healthcare, and cities. This process of "detaching from the carrier and building a network" is the core logic of intelligence becoming infrastructure.

The Infrastructuralization of Intelligence: The "New Energy Network" for the Data Age

If power systems are "networks for energy flow," then intelligent systems are "networks for data processing"—this network is enabling intelligent technology to break free from single devices and become an infrastructure that permeates all scenarios. What we see today, from ChatGPT and smartwatches to autonomous driving, are essentially "terminal interfaces" of this network, not intelligence itself. The true intelligent infrastructure is a "data processing system" composed of four core components: cloud computing centers (such as the server clusters of Alibaba Cloud and Amazon Web Services), IoT sensor networks (traffic cameras and home sensors across cities), data transmission networks (5G and fiber optics), and AI algorithm models (such as Transformer and deep learning frameworks).

The core function of this system is to realize "real-time data collection, efficient processing, and intelligent feedback," providing undifferentiated "intelligent support" for all scenarios.

In urban scenarios, the "City Brain" is a typical manifestation of the infrastructuralization of intelligence. Hangzhou's City Brain is not a single smart device but a city-wide 'data processing network': traffic cameras capture road conditions, 5G transmits the data, AI calculates decisions, and traffic lights execute them. Simply put, it is not a "single intelligent device" but the "underlying network" that makes the entire city "smart."

In home scenarios, the "pervasive nature" of intelligent infrastructure is more intuitive. Today's smart homes are far beyond "individual device intelligence" (like a Wi-Fi-enabled AC or a voice-controlled light); they represent "system-level intelligence." A smart gateway acts as the "data hub," connecting all devices—mattress, AC, curtains, refrigerator. Sensors collect human sleep data (turning frequency, heart rate) and environmental data (temperature, humidity, light levels). AI algorithms analyze this data to automatically adjust curtain opening/closing times (based on sunrise and sleep state), AC temperature (based on human metabolism), and send fridge replenishment reminders (based on remaining ingredients). In this scenario, the user does not "use" a single smart device but "lives" within an environment constructed by the intelligent system—there's no need to manually adjust the AC because the system has already optimized the temperature based on sleep state; no need to remember to buy milk because the system has sent a reminder based on fridge inventory. This kind of "imperceptible support" is the hallmark of intelligence as infrastructure—just as we don't "use" electricity but simply enjoy the conveniences it enables, we may not need to actively "use" intelligence but simply live comfortably within an environment shaped by it.

The essence of this infrastructuralization is the shift of "intelligence from a 'tool attribute' to an 'environmental attribute'." Early intelligent devices, like voice assistants from the 1990s, were essentially "tools"—the user had to issue active commands (e.g., "play music") for the device to act. Today's intelligent infrastructure is essentially an "environment"—it proactively senses user needs (via sleep data, behavior habits) and proactively adjusts the environmental state (optimizing temperature, reminding to restock). The interaction between user and intelligence shifts from "active operation" to "natural integration." This transition marks the point where intelligent technology completely breaks through the boundary of "individual tool" to become a "foundation for existence," like air, water, and electricity—it is no longer merely a means for humans to transform the world but part of the human environment itself.

The Deeper Impact of the Paradigm Shift: When Intelligence Becomes "The Environment Itself"

The paradigm shift of intelligence from "individual tool" to "civilizational infrastructure" has profound implications that extend far beyond increased convenience in daily life; it reconfigures the fundamental relationships between humans and technology, and between humans and their environment. Before the electrical revolution, humanity's relationship with energy was one of "active acquisition"—to obtain energy, one had to chop wood, burn coal, operate a steam engine. After electricity became infrastructure, the relationship transformed into "passive enjoyment"—simply plug into the grid to receive energy indiscriminately. This shift in relationship allowed humans to devote more energy to creation (like scientific research, artistic endeavor) rather than to energy acquisition.

Today, humanity's relationship with intelligence is undergoing a similar transformation: from "active tool use" to "passive integration into the environment." Before the emergence of intelligent infrastructure, humans had to actively operate computers, search the web, and input commands to process data and obtain information. As intelligence becomes infrastructure, humans receive the support of intelligent systems without active operation—navigation apps automatically avoid traffic jams, intelligent medical systems proactively remind us of check-ups, smart education systems adapt to learning paces automatically. This "immersive quality" leads to a reduction in human cognitive load and a restructuring of our way of life: we no longer need to memorize vast amounts of information (delegated to intelligent systems for storage), nor spend significant time on basic decisions (delegated to intelligent systems for optimization), allowing us to focus our energies on matters requiring greater creativity and human warmth—such as emotional connection, value contemplation, and civilizational exploration.

Yet this paradigm shift also prompts new questions: When intelligence becomes the environment itself, how do we define "our own subjectivity"? Just as electricity made humanity dependent on the power grid, intelligent infrastructure makes us dependent on data processing networks—if a navigation app fails, we might get lost; if an intelligent medical system misses a diagnosis, treatment might be delayed. This dependency is not inherently bad, but it demands that we reconsider: within an environment constructed by intelligence, what is the core value of humanity? Should we continue to hold onto "basic decision-making capabilities," or delegate these to the system, focusing instead on values the system cannot replace (like creativity, empathy, ethical judgment)?

These questions are precisely the deeper significance of intelligence as the "new electricity"—it is not merely a technological revolution but also a moment of self-reflection for human civilization. The electrical revolution freed humanity from the constraints of "energy acquisition," leading to modern civilization. The intelligent revolution may free humanity from the constraints of "basic decision-making," paving the way for a more creative civilizational form. Yet, no matter how technology evolves, the essence of infrastructure remains "serving humanity"—electricity serves human energy needs, intelligence serves human data processing needs, both ultimately pointing towards "human well-being and civilizational progress." Understanding the infrastructural nature of intelligence allows us to avoid being dazzled by individual technological marvels and instead see the direction of the intelligent revolution more clearly: to make intelligence the "invisible skeleton" supporting humanity's pursuit of higher values, not the "dominant force" defining the meaning of human existence. This is the core insight that intelligence, as the "new electricity," offers to humanity.

Section 4: The Starting Point of Subjectivity: Defining the "Self" When Intelligence Becomes the "Environment"

As intelligent technology completes its leap from "passive tool" to "active ecological element," and as data processing capabilities permeate every crevice of our homes, transportation, and healthcare like electricity, our focus shifts from "how to use intelligence" to "how to exist within an environment constructed by intelligence." This reconfiguration of the living scenario quietly shakes the "foundation of self-cognition" established over millennia of human civilization—subjectivity. From the absolute dominance of primitive humans using stone tools to cut meat in the Great Rift Valley, to our current reliance on intelligent recommendations for reading choices and smart homes to adjust life's rhythms, the belief that "humans are the masters of their own actions and environment" faces a systematic challenge for the first time. The mission of this chapter is not to provide a standard answer for "how to safeguard subjectivity," but to pry open the intellectual fissure hidden behind "intelligent convenience": When tools become the environment, when technology begins to shape human choices and cognition in reverse, where are the boundaries of the "self"? Does "autonomous will" still exist? These questions are the key to understanding the deep impact of the intelligent revolution and the intellectual starting point for this book's exploration of "how humanity can lead change."

The Millennia-Long Foundation of Subjectivity: The "Human-Tool" Relationship and Self-Definition in the Traditional Tool Era

To grasp the disruptive nature of the "loosening of subjectivity" in the intelligent age, we must first look back into history to see how the "human-tool" relationship of the traditional tool era fortified the definition of the "self." Since the dawn of humanity, tools have always been a "mirror for self-cognition"—through the process of using tools to transform the world, humans confirmed their identity as "active agents" and drew a clear boundary between the "self" and the "external world." This relationship formed the millennia-long skeleton of human subjectivity.

From an anthropological perspective, the use of early tools directly shaped the cognition of "human as the dominant force." In the Oldowan tool era, when a primitive human grasped and swung a stone tool to obtain food, the process followed a chain: "human intention" (the need to cut meat) was the starting point, the "tool's action" (the blade cutting) was the execution, and the "change in the world" (the separated meat) was the result. These three formed a one-way chain: Human → Tool → World. The tool had no independent will, could not deviate from human intention, and certainly could not demand adjustments from the human. This closed loop of "intention-execution-result" gave early humans their first sense of the power of the "self"—through the tool, "I" could make the world change according to "my will." This sense of power was the most primitive germination of "self-subjectivity." As tools evolved, this relationship never changed. The Neolithic farmer wielding a stone axe decided how to sharpen it, controlled the rhythm of chopping, and determined the use of the felled trees. The industrial-age worker operating a steam engine regulated its speed via valves, controlled its start/stop with a switch, and planned the use of its products. In these scenarios, the tool was always an "extended limb" or "amplified force," its value entirely dependent on human intention. Humans, through their control of tools, continually reinforced the self-cognition of "I am the initiator, the decider, the master of my actions."

From a philosophical dimension, this "human-tool" relationship underpinned the core of modern Western subjectivity. Descartes' "Cogito, ergo sum" placed "rational thought" as the ultimate proof of "self-existence"—precisely because humans could define needs, set goals, and control tools through reason, the "self" possessed an unshakable subjectivity. Kant, in his Critique of Practical Reason, emphasized "free will," arguing that human morality and value stem from "autonomous choice free from external coercion." In the traditional tool era, tools were the very antithesis of "external coercion"—they only executed human choices, imposing no coercion. This subjectivity, characterized by "rational dominance and free will," peaked in the industrial age. Even workers on a Ford assembly line, performing repetitive motions, remained the "masters" of the production process—they decided when to start the machine, how to inspect the product, whether to pause production. A housewife using a washing machine, even as automation increased, remained the "definer of needs"—she chose the wash cycle, decided when to start, how to hang the clothes. In the logic of traditional tools, the "self" was the absolute center, and tools were "assistants" revolving around it. This relationship was never overturned.

More fundamentally, the boundary between "human" and "tool" in the traditional era was clear, and this boundary served as a reference point for the "self's" territory. An axe, when in use, is an "extension of the hand," but when set down, becomes an object separate from the "self." A washing machine, while running, is a "household helper," but when unplugged, loses its connection to the "self." The relationship between tool and "self" was one of "separable collaboration"— humans could interrupt the interaction at any time, returning to a pure "tool-less" self. This "separability" allowed humans to always clearly perceive: "I" am "me," the tool is the "tool." The "self" would not be altered or consumed by tool use. As philosopher Martin Buber distinguished between "I-Thou" and "I-It" relationships, the tool is an "It," an object for human cognition and use, while the "I" is the cognizing and utilizing subject. Their statuses never reversed.

This millennia-constant "human-tool" relationship provided a stable coordinate system for human self-definition: The "self" is a being with reason, will, and the ability to its own actions and environment; tools are the means to realize the "self's" intentions. When intelligent technology shatters this relationship, turning tools into a life-permeating environment, this coordinate system begins to tilt—the definition of the "self" loses its familiar reference points for the first time.

Anticipation and Choice: When Intelligence "Thinks Ahead" for Us, Does Autonomous Will Remain?

The first challenge intelligent environments pose to subjectivity comes from their "anticipatory capacity"—they no longer wait for human commands but actively perceive needs, plan solutions in advance, and even execute decisions directly. When a smart fridge automatically detects low milk and places an order, when a navigation app directly plots the "optimal route" without us comparing options, when a recommendation system pushes "content you might like" without active searching, the "autonomous choice" we take for granted becomes blurred. The core of this blurring is not "losing the right to choose," but "losing the necessityand autonomyof choice"—when intelligence has already "thought ahead" for us, does our "choice" still belong to a genuine autonomous will?

The "Being-Defined" of Needs: When Anticipation Replaces "Active Perception"

The starting point of autonomous will is "actively perceiving one's own needs"—knowing "what I need" is the prerequisite for "what I choose." The anticipatory capacity of intelligent environments is quietly shifting this starting point from the "human self" to the "technological system." A Samsung Family Hub smart fridge, using internal cameras to identify ingredient inventory and combining it with user consumption records, can automatically generate a "shopping list" sent to the user's phone, or even place orders directly on linked e-commerce platforms. Superficially, this is "convenience"— the user no longer needs to remember inventory or manually order. But from a subjectivity perspective, the "right to perceive needs" has been partially transferred: the user no longer confirms a need through active perception ("opening the fridge to find the milk is gone") but learns of the need through the system's "reminder." More subtly, the system's "anticipatory logic" quietly defines needs—if the system defaults "2 cartons of milk per week" as "normal need," even if the user wants to reduce intake due to dietary changes, the reminder may still come, reinforcing the cognition of "I need to consume as the system expects," gradually making the user's need perception reliant on the system's judgment. This phenomenon of "needs being defined" is more common in digital spaces. ByteDance's recommendation algorithm, by analyzing user browsing time, likes, and comments, can accurately anticipate "content of potential interest" and present it directly in a "feed." The user, upon opening the app, doesn't actively search for "what I want to see"; the algorithm has already "defined" the need. This "hand-fed" satisfaction of needs causes users to gradually lose the ability to "actively explore needs." When "what I need" stems not from active self-perception but from a system's anticipatory push, the foundation of "autonomous will" begins to loosen.

The "Being-Delimited" of Choice: When Algorithms Frame the "Range of Options"

Even if we can actively perceive a need, the "personalized recommendations" of intelligent environments quietly delimit the range of choices, turning "autonomous choice" into "selecting from algorithm-framed options." Amazon's product recommendation system acts as an "invisible shopping guide"—when a user searches for "sneakers," the system doesn't show all available options but filters down to 20-30 items the "algorithm deems the user most likely to buy" based on spending power, style preference, and browsing history. The user feels they are making an "autonomous choice," but the scope was predetermined. This is the essence of the "algorithmic filter bubble"'s influence on autonomous will. As American author Eli Pariser illustrated in The Filter Bubble, algorithms create a personalized "bubble" for each user. This bubble acts like a transparent wall—it wraps the user inside, allowing them to see mostly what they like, while hiding divergent views outside. When choices are consistently confined within the bubble, "autonomous choice" becomes an illusion.

The "Being-Simplified" of Decision: When Intelligence "Bears Responsibility" for Us

The core of autonomous will is not just "choosing what," but also "taking responsibility for the choice"—it is precisely because we bear the consequences that we deliberate before choosing and feel the "self's" control over actions. The "decision support" of intelligent environments quietly simplifies the process of "taking responsibility," creating a buffer between the "self" and the "consequences of actions." The "automatic emergency braking" in smart driving systems can brake to avoid a collision without driver input. From a safety perspective, this is progress; "decision responsibility" is partially transferred. If the system misjudges, the driver may blame "system failure" rather than their own late reaction. This "transfer of responsibility" causes humans to gradually lose direct of the link between action and consequence. When intelligent systems bear part of the decision-making responsibility, our confidence in the "self's" control over actions weakens.

The Dissolution of Boundaries: From "Tool Extension" to "Environmental Integration," How is the Territory of the Self Demarcated?

If the challenges to "anticipation and choice" target the "autonomous will" of subjectivity, then the "dissolution of human-machine boundaries" targets the "territory of the self." When intelligence is no longer a "separable tool" but an "inseparable environment," when smart prosthetics convey touch, AI assistants understand emotions, and brain-computer interfaces connect thoughts, where are the boundaries of the "self"? What distinguishes "human" from "technology"? This dissolution of boundaries is more fundamental—it directly shakes the physiological and cognitive foundations of "what it means to be human."

The Blurring of Bodily Boundaries: From "Tool Assistance" to "Functional Replacement"

Traditional tools extended the body only at the level of "assistance"—a cane aids walking but doesn't replace the legs' function. The relationship was "external assistance" with clear boundaries. Intelligent technology is breaking through "assistance" to "functional replacement" or even "enhancement," blurring bodily boundaries. A smart prosthetic limb with sensory feedback can make the user "feel" the ground pressure, making it feel less like an "external tool" and more like "part of the body." Brain-computer interface technology is even more disruptive: when brain signals can directly interact with external devices, the definition of the "body" is rewritten. The physical boundary of the "bodily self" expands.

The Blurring of Cognitive Boundaries: From "Tool-Assisted Thinking" to "Tool-Participatory Thinking"

Traditional tools assisted cognition at the level of "information storage and calculation"—a book stores knowledge but doesn't participate in thinking. Intelligent technology is breaking through "support" to "participation," blurring cognitive boundaries. Large language models like ChatGPT don't just store knowledge; they participate in the human thinking process. This "participatory thinking" makes the intelligent tool a "cognitive partner" rather than just an assistant. Furthermore, intelligent technology is changing human cognitive habits through "cognitive outsourcing" (e.g., navigation, AI writing), leading to a potential loss of basic cognitive abilities and a growing dependence on technological tools. The boundary of the "cognitive self" dissolves in this dependency.

The Blurring of Social Boundaries: From "Tool-Assisted Socializing" to "Tool as Social Agent"

Traditional tools assisted social interaction as "communication channels"—a phone connects people but isn't the social object itself. Intelligent technology is breaking through the "medium" to become the "social object," blurring social boundaries. AI assistants like Microsoft's Xiaoice can engage in emotional exchanges, leading users to form emotional attachments. The rise of virtual idols further dissolves social boundaries. When the social object can be an "algorithmically generated virtual image," the definition of the "social self" is rewritten.

Questioning, Not Answers: The Possibility of Reconstructing Subjectivity through Interaction

After examining the "loosening of autonomous will" and the "dissolution of self-boundaries," it's easy to fall into a pessimistic view that intelligent technology is eroding human subjectivity. But this pessimism overlooks the nature of subjectivity—it has never been a "static, absolute dominance," but rather a "dynamic process constantly reconstructed through interaction with the external world." The possibility of reconstruction lies, first, in "human reflective capacity"—our ability to recognize the challenge allows us to actively adjust our interaction with technology. Secondly, it lies in the "malleability of technology"—intelligent systems are not immutable laws but human-designed systems whose values can be shaped. If "human subjectivity" becomes a core design value, we can create systems that support rather than undermine it.

Ultimately, the questioning of subjectivity in the intelligent age is essentially a question about "how human civilization can co-evolve with technology." The evolution of intelligent technology from tool to environment is not meant to replace humanity but to co-construct richer living scenarios. In these scenarios, the definition of the "self" might shift from "absolute master" to "collaborator interacting with technology"; the connotation of "subjectivity" might evolve from a "pure self independent of technology" to "the ability to realize self-worth through interaction with technology." This shift is not a loss of subjectivity, but its evolution.

The questioning in this chapter ends here, but it is not the conclusion; it is the starting point for the book's reflection. Carrying the question of "how the self is defined" into the subsequent discussions about the "body revolution," "cognitive captive," and "civilizational choices" will allow us to see more clearly that the true challenge of the intelligent revolution lies not in the technology itself, but in whether humanity can anchor the "value of the self" amidst the technological tide.

The Spatial Revolution:
Future Dwellings

1. The Paradigm Shift: From "Remote-Controlled Tools" to "Residential Ecosystem"

2. The Health Guardian: The Underlying Logic of the Dwelling as a Personal Caretaker

3. Emotion and Companionship: When Space Possesses "Warmth"

4. The Privacy Protection Dilemma in the Flow of Data

5. The Return to the Essence of "People-Oriented" Future Dwellings

Chapter 2
The Spatial Revolution: Future Dwellings

The concept of "home"—humanity's most ancient sanctuary—is being fundamentally rewritten by technology. It is no longer a passive assemblage of remote-controlled tools awaiting commands, but has evolved into a living, breathing, perceiving entity that grows alongside us. When walls learn to observe, mattresses understand care, and lighting possesses mood, what we gain is not just ultimate convenience, but an unprecedented experience of being "understood by our environment." This chapter explores this shift in spatial paradigm and confronts its core paradox of warmth: When the home itself becomes an attentive "guardian of health and emotion," are we building a more secure harbor, or ceding our last frontier of privacy to a gentle guardian with watchful eyes?

Section 1: The Paradigm Shift: From "Remote-Controlled Tools" to "Residential Ecosystem"

Throughout the long river of human civilization, living spaces have always been the cornerstone of our survival and development. From the initial caves providing shelter from wind and rain to today's towering skyscrapers, the forms and functions of dwellings have undergone countless transformations. Today, a profound revolution is unfolding around us – one that seeks to redefine the very meaning of "home." Home is transitioning from a set of manually operated "remote-controlled tools" into a vibrant "residential ecosystem" capable of responding to our needs.

Glimpses of this transformation are already visible in real-world applications. For instance, using platforms like Apple HomeKit or Xiaomi's Mi Home, simply saying "I'm almost home" before arrival can trigger the system to automatically adjust the air conditioning to a comfortable temperature, turn on warm lighting, and prepare hot water. This seamless integration between scenarios is a vivid demonstration of how the "residential ecosystem" surpasses the "remote-controlled tool."

Looking back, the prototypes of smart homes were merely devices that could be simply controlled via remote controls or smartphones, such as smart bulbs allowing us to change light colors from the sofa, or smart curtains that opened and closed with one tap. At that time, we viewed these devices as "remote-controlled tools" enhancing life convenience. They operated in isolation, acting only upon explicit commands. Take early smart speakers as an example: users primarily employed them to play music or check the weather – their functions were limited to executing single tasks, like an obedient but lacking-initiative servant.

With the rapid advancement of technologies like the Internet of Things (IoT) and artificial intelligence (AI), the situation has changed dramatically. Today, various smart devices are beginning to break down silos and connect through unified platforms. Smart home ecosystems represented by Apple's HomeKit, Huawei's HarmonyOS, and Xiaomi's Mi Home are like installing a powerful "operating system" for our homes. Under this system, devices like lights, air conditioners, speakers, and refrigerators seem endowed with the ability to communicate and begin working in concert. Imagine this: on your way home from work, you tell your smart home system via phone, "I'm almost home." Instantly, the home air conditioner automatically adjusts to a suitable temperature, lights turn on in a warm hue, the water heater starts warming up, and speakers play your favorite relaxing music. This is no longer simple device control; it's proactive service from a system based on your habits and needs.

From a technical perspective, this shift stems from the realization of data exchange and sharing between devices. Each smart device acts like a neuron within an ecosystem, continuously collecting information, transmitting signals, and learning your behavioral patterns and preferences through algorithms. A smart camera recognizes a family member, triggers the door lock to open automatically, and simultaneously relays this information to other devices to initiate a personalized "welcome home" scenario. Thus, the home evolves from a static physical space into a dynamically responsive organic whole.

Analyzing from the perspective of fundamental human biological instincts, humans inherently seek convenience and comfort. This transition from "remote-controlled tools" to an "intelligent ecosystem" greatly satisfies this basic need. It liberates us from tedious device operations, freeing up time and energy to invest in more meaningful activities like spending time with family or developing personal interests.

Different cultures hold unique understandings and expectations of "home," and the development of smart homes is intertwining with these cultural traditions, reshaping our perception of living spaces. In Eastern cultures, home is often regarded as an emotional anchor and the core of family heritage. In Japan, for example, the traditional "washitsu" culture emphasizes harmonious coexistence with nature, pursuing a tranquil, simple living atmosphere. Today, Japan's smart home development incorporates this cultural concept, yielding many designs focused on detail and inspired by natural elements. For instance, some smart lights can simulate sunrise and sunset light changes, creating a rhythm synchronized with nature; smart air purification systems automatically adjust based on indoor and outdoor environments, maintaining fresh air akin to being in a forest. Such designs not only meet the convenience demands of modern life but also carry forward the Japanese cultural spirit of reverence for and integration with nature.

In Chinese culture, the concept of home is closely linked with "reunion" and "harmony." Smart home manufacturers have keenly captured this, developing features conducive to family interaction and emotional connection. For example, some smart TVs function as family entertainment hubs, supporting multi-player online games and video calls, allowing family members to share joyful moments through the screen even when apart. Smart family photo albums can automatically organize family photos and play them on a loop on the living room screen, evoking fond memories and strengthening family bonds. Philosophically, this reflects the Eastern idea of "harmony between man and nature," merging technology with humanity and nature, making home not just a physical space but a spiritual sanctuary carrying emotions and cultural memory.

As social structures evolve, with the proliferation of dual-income families and accelerated pace of life, the convenience of smart homes becomes increasingly precious. Family health management serves as an example: smart bracelets and blood pressure monitors track family members' health in real-time, syncing data to the home system. If abnormal blood pressure is detected in an elderly person, the system immediately notifies family members and can even automatically contact community doctors. Smart kitchen appliances can recommend recipes and assist with cooking based on health data and dietary preferences. Thus, the home upgrades from a mere living quarters to a comprehensive life support center.

Simultaneously, the growing population of people living alone is reshaping the social landscape. Smart doorbells become the "electronic eyes" for elderly individuals living alone, allowing them to safely verify visitors without leaving home; smart speakers become "emotional confidants" for young people late at night, offering a healing melody or a warm joke in moments of loneliness. These technological products not only fill the emotional gaps left by changing family structures but also gently maintain the emotional bond between people and their living spaces.

When we examine this shift from a philosophical height, it signifies a fundamental reshaping of the relationship between people and their dwellings. In traditional views, dwellings were tools created by humans to meet survival needs, over which we held absolute control. However, with the development of smart homes, this relationship has become more complex and nuanced. When our homes can perceive our behaviors and emotions through sensors, even predicting our needs, the dwelling ceases to be merely a passive object and begins to possess a degree of subjectivity. It becomes like a sentient partner, engaging in a silent dialogue with us. This change prompts us to reconsider the essence of "home" and our role within it. Heidegger proposed the concept of "poetically dwelling" – that human existence on earth should not merely be material survival but a "poetic" way of harmoniously coexisting with nature and the world. In the current era of smart homes, this ideal is gradually becoming reality. Through the integration of technology and humanity, our dwellings are no longer cold accumulations of building materials but are filled with vitality and warmth, becoming an important part of our life's meaning.

However, shadows inevitably accompany the light. As our lives become increasingly reliant on this seamless, automated ecosystem, a new form of "systemic dependency" quietly emerges. A network outage or a minor system bug could throw our entire life rhythm into disarray. Will we, like the humans floating in the spaceship in WALL-E, dull certain innate life skills and perceptions amidst ultimate comfort? Will we still remember how to manually adjust a thermostat valve? Will we instinctively add clothing for a family member when the weather turns cold, rather than waiting for a system notification? This is not a call to reject technology, but a reminder: while enjoying the "effortless life" offered by the ecosystem, we must retain the awareness and ability for a life that requires effort. We cannot relinquish all initiative in living. The ultimate purpose of technology is empowerment, not deprivation; to make us more capable "humans," not regress into "appendages" of the system.

The shift from "remote-controlled tools" to a "residential ecosystem" is far more than technological progress; it is a cognitive revolution, a cultural evolution, and a philosophical practice. It is redefining the meaning of "home": home is no longer just a physical shelter, a container filled with appliances, but a living entity that can breathe, perceive, grow, and engage in deep interaction with its inhabitants. Our relationship with it also evolves from one-way "control-obedience" to two-way "dialogue-symbiosis." We shape its habits, and it, in turn, subtly shapes our lifestyle and our way of perceiving the world.

In this grand paradigm shift, we are both designers and experiencers, both beneficiaries and, necessarily,a clear-headed thinker. Because, ultimately, what we must safeguard is not the seamlessness and dazzle of the technology, but the genuine autonomy, warmth, and humanity that belong to "home."

Section 2: The Health Guardian: The Underlying Logic of the Dwelling as a Personal Caretaker

In humanity's eternal pursuit of longevity and health, the dwelling has always played the role of a silent guardian. Today, intelligent technology is pushing this ancient vision to unprecedented heights— the home is evolving from a passive shelter into an active, ubiquitous "health guardian." Behind this transformation lies the deep integration of data, algorithms, and human needs, bringing the dawn of precise care while also provoking profound reflection on the boundaries of healthcare and the potential alienation of humanity.

Intelligent health monitoring has quietly entered households. For example, a smart mattress can non-intrusively monitor a user's sleep heart rate and respiration. Upon detecting abnormal fluctuations, it can automatically trigger the air conditioner to adjust the room temperature and offer a gentle reminder via a smart speaker in the morning to rest. This closed loop of "perception-analysis-intervention" is the core logic of the dwelling as a health manager.

The health-guarding capability of the intelligent dwelling is not the result of a single technology but is built upon a tightly connected three-layer technical architecture: "Perception – Analysis – Intervention." This structure endows the dwelling with "eyes to perceive the external world," a "brain to think and judge," and "hands to take action," achieving a complete closed loop from data collection to proactive guardianship through the coordinated operation of all levels.

In the Perception Layer, various sensors distributed throughout the living space act like "neural endpoints," continuously capturing key data to provide the foundational information for health guarding. For instance, non-contact sleep sensors installed by the bedroom headboard can collect real-time sleep data like heart rate, respiration rate, and toss-and-turn frequency; environmental sensors in the living room and bedroom monitor indoor temperature, humidity, PM2.5 levels, formaldehyde concentration, and other metrics; smart blood pressure monitors and body fat scales in the bathroom automatically record physiological data like blood pressure and body fat percentage during daily use; smart food recognition sensors in the kitchen can even assess the freshness and nutritional content of ingredients. These sensors integrate seamlessly into daily life without requiring deliberate user operation, continuously aggregating dynamic data on both the environment and the occupants.

Once data is collected, it enters the Analysis Layer—the "brain center" of the intelligent dwelling. Data from the perception layer is transmitted in real-time via IoT technology to the home central control system, where built-in machine learning algorithms perform deep processing. Consider a household with an elderly resident suffering from hypertension. The central system compares daily blood pressure data from the smart monitor against the individual's historical health records (such as past blood pressure fluctuation patterns and medication history). If the algorithm identifies blood pressure readings consistently exceeding the normal range for three consecutive mornings, and cross-references this with data from environmental sensors indicating "low indoor temperature at night," it quickly deduces that "the abnormal blood pressure may be related to insufficient warmth at night." It further predicts the potential risk of symptoms like dizziness or chest tightness within the next 24 hours, simultaneously generating preliminary suggestions such as "adjust the nighttime indoor temperature to 22°C" and "remind to take antihypertensive medication on time."

Finally, the Intervention Layer translates the analysis layer's conclusions into concrete actions, completing the health guardianship loop. The system synchronously triggers multiple interventions: it pushes alerts and health suggestions to the children's mobile phones; directly controls the bedroom air conditioner to set the nighttime temperature to 22°C; and uses the bedside speaker to offer a voice reminder in the morning: "Please measure your blood pressure and take your medication." If the data continues to be suboptimal, the system can integrate with the TV, popping up an option: "Would you like to contact your family doctor?" thus simplifying the process of seeking help.

It is precisely through this three-tier architecture of "data sensing → analysis and judgment → active intervention" that the intelligent dwelling upgrades from a mere "data logger" collecting information to a "health manager" capable of accurately identifying health risks and proactively providing solutions, truly achieving round-the-clock, intelligent guardianship over the occupants' health.

This system's rapid integration into modern life stems from its precise response to two fundamental human needs: the craving for a sense of security and the pursuit of autonomous living. For chronic disease patients and the elderly, this technology brings unprecedented peace of mind. A smart refrigerator for a diabetic can automatically identify the sugar content of food and offer dietary suggestions; a smart bathroom mirror cabinet with a built-in blood pressure monitor allows a hypertensive patient to complete daily checks while washing up. This seamless integration of health management into daily routine ensures safety while maximally preserving individual dignity and autonomy. However, this meticulous monitoring also harbors the risk of alienation. When health management turns into constant data surveillance, when every morsel of food and every step is quantified and evaluated, does life become a perpetual health performance exam? In the pursuit of perfect health data, do we lose the ability to listen to our body's instinctive voices?

The development of intelligent health dwellings also reveals interesting cultural convergence. Influenced by the Western medical tradition, systems often emphasize precise quantification and targeted intervention, reflecting the analytical and reductionist traditions of Western medicine. Simultaneously, systems are quietly incorporating the holistic and preventive views of Eastern wisdom. Some advanced systems now focus on the "harmonious unity of environment and the human body," automatically adjusting indoor humidity and temperature according to seasonal changes. Some smart dwellings in Japan even introduce the "forest bathing" concept, simulating a forest therapy environment within urban apartments by releasing phytoncide-negative ions and playing nature sounds. This health management approach, blending Eastern and Western medical wisdom, signifies that intelligent dwellings are becoming innovative platforms where different cultural health concepts converge.

Against the backdrop of an aging population and uneven distribution of medical resources, intelligent health dwellings are catalyzing profound social change. They effectively shift parts of healthcare functions from hospitals to homes, alleviating pressure on public health systems. The combination of remote consultation systems and home health monitoring devices enables residents in remote areas to access quality medical resources.

Concurrently, intelligent dwellings are redefining caregiving relationships among family members. As technology takes over daily health monitoring and emergency handling tasks, adult children are freed from frequent "check-in" calls, instead focusing on their parents' actual condition through shared health data reports. This shift partially liberates family members from trivial monitoring duties, potentially transforming family care away from a tense dynamic of "monitor and be monitored." Yet risks remain: when technology intervenes too deeply, could it reduce actual contact between family members? Could data reports replace warm touches and face-to-face greetings? This is the ethical paradox that intelligent health guardianship must confront.

The evolution of the intelligent dwelling into a health guardian ultimately forces us to rethink the nature and boundaries of medicine. French philosopher Michel Foucault proposed the concept of the "medical gaze"—where traditional medicine establishes authority and control by objectifying and datafying the body. Today, this "gaze" is encoded into our most private living spaces, becoming a ubiquitous, gentle surveillance. Intelligent health systems promise a utopian vision of "prevention over cure,"but this also means our health status is perpetually being assessed, managed and optimized. Health ceases to be a natural state and becomes a project requiring continuous technical maintenance. When the home itself becomes a means of medical intervention, is its attribute as a "refuge" for relaxation and escape from social pressures being diminished?

The ultimate paradox of intelligent health guardianship lies here: it immensely enhances an individual's ability to control their own health, yet simultaneously cedes health management authority to algorithms and systems. The core issue for the concept of health in the intelligent age is how to enjoy the sense of security brought by technology while preventing the "alienation" of health management and safeguarding human autonomy and integrity. True health guardianship perhaps lies not in how precisely technology can monitor our physiological metrics, but in whether it can help us better understand and accept the natural processes of life—including those feelings that cannot be quantified, the inevitable decline, and the vulnerabilities and imperfections that define our humanity. The health mission of the intelligent dwelling should not be to create flawless "superhumans," but to support every ordinary person in living their own, complete life in an environment of dignity and warmth.

Section 3: Emotion and Companionship: When Space Possesses "Warmth"

Home has never been merely a physical space built of brick and concrete; it is a container of memories, a harbor for emotions, a silent witness to countless moments of joy and vulnerability in life. Amid the wave of the intelligent revolution, this most intimate space is learning a new skill: attempting to understand and respond to our deep-seated yearning for companionship and resonance. As cold algorithms reach out, trying to touch the warmest emotional realms of humanity, a silent experiment concerning technology, loneliness, and intimacy is quietly underway in millions of households.

The emotional turn of the intelligent dwelling is technically founded on the convergence of ambient intelligence and affective computing. Through sensors and microphones distributed throughout the space, the system can capture the occupant's behavioral patterns, vocal inflections, and even subtle changes in facial expressions. AI analyzes these multimodal data streams to infer the user's emotional state—be it joy, fatigue, anxiety, or loneliness. Based on this understanding, the system proactively triggers corresponding interactions: dimming the lights and playing soothing music upon detecting low spirits; suggesting contacting a friend or recommending online community activities when sensing loneliness. This shift from passive response to active empathy marks the evolution of smart homes from functional tools towards emotional partners.

Loneliness has become an epidemic in modern society. Elderly people living alone spend long days and nights in front of the TV; young urbanites yearn for sincere connection in cramped apartments; high-intensity workers feel a sense of loss when facing empty rooms after work—these scenes form the normalized landscape of contemporary life.Amid this context, intelligent technology has stepped in at the right time to address this emotional vacuum, attempting to fill the gaps in human connection. Voice assistants remember users' birthdays and send greetings; smart robotic pets provide unconditional companionship to elderly people living alone; avatar technology allows relatives far away to "appear" in family spaces in a more tangible form. While these technological solutions cannot fully replace human intimate relationships, they have somewhat alleviated the loneliness brought by modernity, becoming an indispensable emotional support in the daily lives of countless people.

However, this "manufactured warmth" also brings sharp philosophical and ethical questions: When algorithms simulate empathy, when machines provide emotional support, are we sliding towards a new form of "emotional alienation"? German philosopher Martin Heidegger warned that technology could frame the world, turning everything, including human relationships, into calculable, manageable resources. Intelligent companionship technology sits at the heart of this risk—it reduces precious human emotional interaction to data input and output, diminishing the complex capacity for empathy to a pattern recognition problem. More disquieting is that this simulated companionship might satisfy people with shallow emotional connections, allowing them to escape the more challenging yet richer realm of real human relationships. Just as social media gives the illusion of connection while potentially exacerbating loneliness, intelligent companionship might create an illusion of being understood, yet fail to provide genuine human resonance.

From a cultural perspective, the acceptance of technology intruding into the emotional domain varies interestingly across societies. In cultures steeped in techno-optimism, people are more willing to embrace intelligent companionship, viewing it as a reasonable extension enhancing human capabilities. The high acceptance of robotic companions in Japanese society is closely related to the traditional cultural concept of "animism," which makes it easier to accept non-human entities as emotional partners. Conversely, in cultures that highly value interpersonal intimacy, the emotional application of technology faces more skepticism, with concerns that it could lead to further commodification and superficiality of human relationships. These cultural differences reveal that technological development is not a value-neutral process but a social construct deeply influenced by specific cultural values and societal needs.

The design of companionship technology also contains profound cultural metaphors and biases. Most voice assistants are given female names and voices,imperceptibly reinforcing the social notion that caregiving and emotional labor are traditionally female roles. Emotion recognition algorithms are often trained on facial expression data from specific cultural groups, leading to significantly reduced accuracy in recognizing emotional expressions from other cultures. Behind these technical details lie cultural assumptions and value judgments that need scrutiny, reminding us that even the most "intelligent" systems struggle to completely escape the cultural limitations and unconscious biases of their designers.

From a developmental psychology standpoint, the impact of intelligent companionship technology on children and adolescents deserves particular attention. The growing generation might take smart assistants for granted as conversational partners. This could foster their comfort with technology but might also impact the development of their human social skills. When children become accustomed to issuing commands to digital assistants, will they learn the subtle etiquette and mutual respect inherent in human conversation? When algorithms constantly adapt to and satisfy all their preferences, will they still develop the necessary skills to handle disagreement and conflict? The answers to these questions will shape the social landscape and emotional patterns of future generations.

Facing these challenges, we need to adopt a stance of critical embrace—acknowledging the positive value of intelligent companionship technology in alleviating modern loneliness while remaining vigilant about its potential for interpersonal alienation and emotional simplification. Technology's true mission should not be to replace human relationships but to enhance our ability to build and maintain genuine connections. The ideal intelligent companionship system should act as a bridge, not a barrier, encouraging users to strengthen real-world interpersonal bonds rather than replace them. For example, the system could remind the user to contact a long-lost friend rather than merely offering algorithm-generated comfort; it could promote shared activities among family members rather than solely providing individualized entertainment.

In an era where technology increasingly permeates the emotional sphere, we need more than ever to return to a fundamental question: what constitutes genuine emotional connection? True empathy is not merely the identification and response to an emotional state; it is the profound acknowledgment of another's uniqueness and subjectivity, the courage to enter another's world and bear emotional risk. These are human qualities difficult for any algorithm to fully replicate. The emotional warmth of an intelligent dwelling should ultimately stem not from the cleverness of its design, but from its ability to facilitate rather than replace those imperfect but real encounters between people, those difficult but sincere conversations, those simple but warm human touches.

Perhaps the most warm-hearted intelligent dwelling is not the one that most accurately simulates companionship, but the space that best helps us become better human partners—a place that reminds us to turn off screens and share a meal, an environment that helps us create beautiful memories rather than merely record data, a home that ultimately makes us more willing to open our hearts rather than close ourselves off. In this vision, technology is not a substitute for emotion but a catalyst for returning to the authenticity of humanity, helping us rediscover and cherish the most basic emotional needs that define us in this rapidly changing digital age.

Section 4: The Privacy Protection Dilemma in the Flow of Data

As the smart home evolves from a mere "functional space" into a complex "data node," a hidden risk surfaces, becoming an inescapable reality: privacy is eroding. From smart mattresses recording your sleep patterns, to smart refrigerators understanding your dietary preferences, and security cameras capturing your movement trajectories within the home—these seemingly fragmented data points, once integrated and analyzed, are sufficient to piece together an extremely intimate panorama of your life. The choice we face is not a simple yes or no to technology, but a difficult balancing act: how to enjoy the convenience brought by intelligence while safeguarding personal privacy.

A data breach incident in a high-end community in Shanghai in late 2023 brought this issue to the forefront. Access records, indoor activity images, and even visitor information of nearly a hundred households were stolen, processed, and turned into "precise user profiles" in the eyes of commercial entities. Some residents found that information about their weekend hours at home and family composition was being used to target them with home cleaning service ads; more alarmingly, a woman living alone received strange calls from someone who knew her daily routine, shattering her sense of security. Such incidents reveal a harsh reality: individual data points might seem insignificant, but once cross-analyzed, they can turn private life into a "transparent fishbowl." As a data security expert pointedly noted: the "functional data" in your eyes can become "risk data" in business logic. Your sleep quality might be linked to insurance premiums, your electricity usage habits could reveal whether you are home. This pervasive uncertainty is the root of modern privacy anxiety

From a technical perspective, privacy risks stem from vulnerabilities throughout the entire data flow, from collection to usage. Many devices engage in "over-collection" from the start, gathering information far beyond what is necessary; transmission often lacks encryption, making data as easy to read as a postcard; during storage and usage stages, insufficient security protection on centralized servers and a lack of oversight regarding third-party data sharing exacerbate leakage risks. A Japanese company was heavily fined for sharing user without authorization indoor data with advertisers; a US smart speaker manufacturer was also exposed for having employees casually listen to user recordings. The tricky part is, data breaches are often characterized by latency and concealment—users typically only discover them after the fact—a sense of powerlessness that further undermines our control over privacy.

The ways people guard their privacy are deeply imprinted by culture. In the Chinese tradition, "family privacy" is a sanctity not to be violated. A survey showed that over 60% of Beijing users refused to install smart cameras in their living rooms and bedrooms, for a simple reason: "Scenes filled with family warmth, like children playing or the elderly cooking, shouldn't become cold data stored on unfamiliar servers." This mindset is also reflected in product design. Domestic smart home brands often promote "local data storage" and "on-device encryption" as key selling points, adapting to the Chinese sensitivity regarding family privacy.

In Europe and the US, however, "individual rights" form the core of privacy protection. The EU's General Data Protection Regulation (GDPR) establishes principles like "data minimization" and the "right to be forgotten," legally endow individuals control over their personal data; California, USA, has passed similar legislation, requiring companies to clearly disclose data usage purposes. However,sound law alone hasn't completely solved the problem—long,obscure user agreement and the high professional threshold required for compliance judgments often leave ordinary people with a helpless choice between "accepting the terms" and "abandoning use," leading to a widespread situation where "rights seem to be in hand, but are practically ceded by necessity."

Privacy issues also involve the complex balance between public and individual interests. During the pandemic, smart monitoring devices provided crucial support for epidemic control but also raised new concerns: must public safety inevitably come at the cost of privacy? Where will this health data go once the emergency ends? Can we ensure it won't be misused? These questions strike at the heart of a key societal governance proposition—how to delineate clear and respected boundaries for personal privacy while safeguarding the public interest.

From a deeper philosophical perspective, the privacy dilemma is essentially a collision between technology and human nature. Human dignity is largely built upon autonomy and private space. As smart devices continuously collect, analyze, and even predict our behavior, this sense of control is quietly diminishing. More disquieting is the psychological "alienation"—one user, whose insurance premiums increased after a health data leak, frankly admitted: "Since knowing my heart rate and step count are being judged, wearing the watch feels like being monitored, even affecting my daily life." This anxiety is not just interest, but fundamental human dignity: we need a private space where we don't have to perform or be on guard—a non-negotiable bottom line in the smart era.

Addressing this dilemma requires joint efforts across multiple dimensions: technology, law, society, and the individual. Technologically, "privacy-enhancing computation" should be promoted, allowing tasks to be completed without directly accessing raw user data, thus achieving "data usability without visibility." Legally, boundaries for data use must be clearly defined, and the cost of violations increased. Societally, public education needs strengthening to raise privacy awareness. And individuals should also authorize rationally, proactively exercise their data rights, and become guardians of their own privacy.

The value of data depends on how we use it. The original purpose of smart homes is to make life better and more relaxed, and privacy protection is precisely the cornerstone of achieving this goal. Only when technology truly respects human dignity and guards the warmth of life will the intelligent era not lose sight of the essence of humanity amid convenience.

Section 5 The Return to the Essence of "People-Oriented" Future Dwellings

Amid the tide of intelligent technology flooding daily life, we were once fascinated by precise algorithms and seamless interactions, as if the ultimate mission of technology was to endlessly optimize efficiency and convenience. Yet as living spaces become increasingly filled with sensors, data streams, and smart devices, a fundamental question gradually emerges: Is the ultimate goal of technology to create a "perfect" environment that requires no human involvement, or to return to people themselves—serving human needs, emotions, and values? The development of smart dwellings is shifting from a technology-driven narrative to a profound return to "people-oriented" principles.

In the early stages of technology, there was always a certain obsession with "intelligence." Manufacturers were eager to demonstrate how to control all household appliances with voice commands and achieve automated scenario linkage, attempting to reshape homes into efficiently operating systems. However, this technology-first mindset overlooked the core point: the essence of a home is a dwelling for people, not a collection of machines. Some families reported having to change long-held living habits to adapt to the "automation" of smart systems; other users complained that "smart scenarios" instead increased operational complexity, making simple tasks cumbersome. Behind these misalignments lies the alienation of technology from a tool to a goal, with humans reduced to objects that adapt to technology. As technology philosopher Lewis Mumford stated: "Over-reliance on technological efficiency will gradually make humans lose control over life itself, becoming vassals to technological logic."

True "people-oriented" design begins with technology respecting diversity and inclusivity. Every family has different living rhythms and member compositions—there is no one-size-fits-all algorithm. An ideal smart system should have the ability to learn and adapt, rather than imposing preset controls. The "Adaptive Scenario System" developed by domestic smart home brand Aqara is quite instructive: users can customize rules through "drag-and-drop operations"—office workers set a "commuting mode" that automatically opens curtains and turns on the coffee machine at 7 a.m.; those working from home set a "focus mode" that disables entertainment notifications and dims lights in non-work areas at 9 a.m. The system also supports "family member permission differentiation": the elderly interface retains only basic functions such as turning lights on/off and adjusting temperature, while the children's interface blocks controls for hazardous devices. This design shift marks the industry's return from "what technology can do" to "what people need," echoing the emphasis by sociologist Anthony Giddens: "Good technology should become an 'empowering tool,' not a 'disciplinary means'; it should provide possibilities for different lifestyles, rather than imposing a single standard."

A deeper level of "people-oriented" design lies in technology's response to emotional and psychological needs. A home is not just a physical container, but also an emotional refuge. Panasonic Japan's 2024 launch of the "Emotion-Resonant Residence" offers a warm solution: through cameras that capture microexpressions and voice modules that analyze tone, if a couple is identified as arguing emotionally, the system automatically warms the lighting, plays soothing music, and pops up a prompt asking, "Would you like to watch an old family video?" If an elderly person living alone is detected remaining silent and immobile for a long time, it simulates the voice of a grandchild to remind them, "The magnolias downstairs are blooming," and pushes community event information. These functions have nothing to do with efficiency, yet they touch the softest parts of the human heart—technology can be more than just a tool for solving problems; it can also be an emotional companion.

In the context of accelerating aging, "people-oriented" design is even more reflected in care for vulnerable groups. According to data from the National Bureau of Statistics, the population of people aged 60 and above in China reached 297 million in 2023. Preventing the elderly from being "marginalized" in the intelligent era is a key task for smart dwellings. The "Age-Appropriate Smart Renovation Project" in Yangpu District, Shanghai, provides valuable references: "Voice-controlled smart handrails" are installed for elderly people with mobility issues—shouting "turn on the light" activates the light and triggers a fall alarm; "tactile switches" are designed for elderly people with declining eyesight, using buttons of different shapes to distinguish devices; most crucially, all devices retain traditional operation methods—for example, smart door locks support both fingerprint recognition and mechanical keys, preventing the elderly from being stranded in case of malfunctions.

For people with disabilities, intelligent technology is even more a pillar of independent living. The "Accessible Smart System" developed by Tencent Cloud in collaboration with public welfare organizations uses eye-tracking technology, allowing users with high paraplegia to control curtains, adjust air conditioning, and send voice messages simply by moving their eyes. These practices confirm the guidelines of the UN Convention on the Rights of Persons with Disabilities: "Technology should promote social inclusion and ensure that all people enjoy the convenience of life on an equal basis—this is the core of technology ethics."

Cultural adaptability is also key to "people-oriented" design. Eastern families emphasize intergenerational cohabitation, so smart homes need to balance the needs of multiple generations; Western families emphasize personal space, so technology must strike a balance between sharing and privacy. The "Garden-Style Smart Residence" in Suzhou integrates Eastern cultural genes: smart screens use Su embroidery craftsmanship, switching patterns representing the four seasons; study lighting simulates changes in natural light, recreating the garden experience of "scenery shifting with each step"; during traditional festivals, the large screen automatically plays old family photos and pushes recipes for dishes loved by elders. The "Nordic-Style Smart Residence" jointly launched by IKEA Sweden and Volvo focuses on symbiosis between humans and nature: smart windows adjust opening and closing based on sunlight, and rainwater is reused for watering plants; the constant temperature system prioritizes ventilation for temperature regulation, aligning with the local habit of "minimizing air conditioning use."

Today, users' attitudes toward technology are also changing. In the early days, they pursued novelty; now, more people are questioning ethical boundaries: Where does data go? Do algorithms manipulate choices? Can technology be "paused" at any time? This awakening is forcing the industry to adopt transparent design. In 2024, Xiaomi's "Privacy-Controllable Smart System" adopted "local-first storage," allowing users to independently choose storage methods and check data records; Huawei's smart speakers added an "algorithm explanation function"—when recommending songs, it explains, "Based on 30 days of folk music playback records and today's weather," instead of the vague "Based on preferences." These changes are building a new technology ethics: intelligence should not be an "invisible controller" that seeps in quietly, but a "thoughtful assistant" that is clearly visible. It ensures users always hold the initiative to choose—neither forcing them to accept preset rules nor concealing data usage, truly making "people" the masters of technology use.

From a philosophical perspective, "people-oriented" smart dwellings re-examine the relationship between technology and humans. Heidegger once warned that technology tends to make humans view the world from a "calculable perspective," yet the significance of a home lies precisely in preserving the unquantifiable aspects: aimless chats, sudden inspirations, and silent contemplation. A family once planned to install a "study monitoring system" in the children's room; the designer suggested adding a "free exploration mode"—turning off monitoring in the evening, activating starry sky lights, and playing natural sounds. Subsequent feedback showed that because children had "daydreaming time," their learning efficiency actually improved. This illustrates that the value of technology is not to eliminate the "uncertainty" of life, but to preserve humans' right to "enjoy uncertainty."

Future smart dwellings may move away from the "fully automated utopia" and toward "symbiotic wisdom": technology handles repetitive tasks and provides safety support, while humans focus on creation and emotional connection. This division of labor is not a step backward, but a sign of technological maturity—understanding boundaries and grasping the essence of service. As Carl Sagan wrote in The Demon-Haunted World: "The best technology is the kind you don't notice, yet it provides just the right help when you need it."

Ultimately, the direction of smart dwellings depends on our answer to "what constitutes a good life"—it has never been a "perfect process" precisely planned by algorithms, but a "real daily life" where one can breathe freely and place emotions at ease. Technology cannot define happiness for us, but it can help us eliminate trivial distractions in life, allowing us to have more energy to embrace each other and preserve memories: it is a light that the elderly can easily turn on, a starry sky under which children can daydream freely, and old family photos that automatically play when the whole family gathers. The intelligent transformation of homes has never been about building a showcase filled with technology, but about nurturing a haven where people can "be themselves with peace of mind"—a space with warmth, memories, and a sense of belonging. We will eventually understand: the smartest home is not the one that best predicts behavior, but the one that best respects human autonomy and accommodates human complexity. It does not pursue cold efficiency, but guards the warmth of daily life; it does not fear the uncertainty of life, but gives people the courage to explore the unknown. This is the deepest empowerment of technology—not to live in place of humans, but to help each person become more vivid and complete versions of themselves.

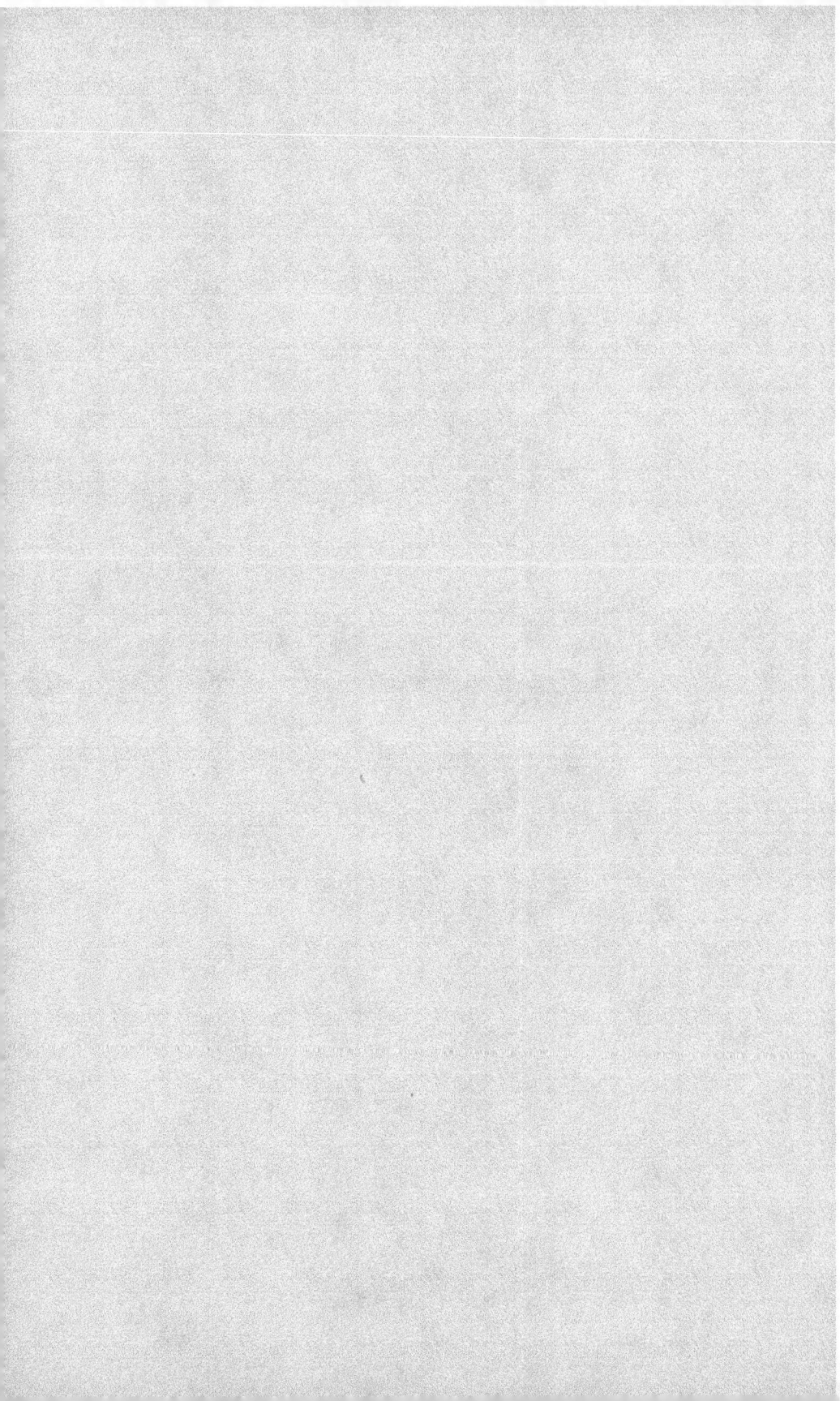

The Body Revolution: Redefining the "Human"

1. The Body's First Layer of "Digital Skin"

2. When Technology "Moves In" to the Body

3. Transcending Nature's "Life Programming"

4. The Definition of "Human" Trembles in the Face of Technology

5. The Essential Return to a "Human-Centered" Future Dwelling

Chapter 3
The Body Revolution: Redefining the "Human"

The integration of technology and humanity is advancing from the superficial "digital skin" deep into the very flesh and blood of our bodies. As chips are implanted within, genes become editable, and consciousness communicates directly with machines, the once self-evident boundaries of the "natural body" begin to blur. We seem to have gained unprecedented control—the ability to repair defects, enhance functions, and even rewrite the fundamental code of life. This chapter delves into this most intimate of revolutions, examining how technology transforms from an external tool into an internal partner, and compelling us to confront an existential question: In this profound fusion with technology, how do we define the "self" constituted by both the "data-driven identity" and the "biological body"? Are we becoming more like gods, or have we lost sight of what it means to be human?

Section 1: The Body's First Layer of "Digital Skin"

In the long history of human-technology symbiosis, we are for the first time so clearly and directly "wearing" technology on our bodies, making it an invisible yet incredibly sensitive layer of "digital skin." This is no longer merely an extension of tools, but almost a proliferation of senses—it listens to heartbeats, senses movement, monitors body temperature, even anticipates mood, translating our biological existence in real-time into data streams that can be read, analyzed, and intervened upon. Wearable devices are quietly reconstructing how we understand our bodies, perceive ourselves, and even our very mode of existence.

For many people, the first thing upon waking is to check their sleep score on a fitness band; during exercise, they rely on their watch to track heart rate zones; they might even stand up and move because of a "sedentary reminder"—this "skin" is silently participating in the rhythm of our every day.

From smartwatches and fitness trackers to smart clothing and electronic tattoos, these devices, despite their varied forms, collectively point to a profound shift: the body is becoming an interface, physiology is becoming information. They record steps, monitor sleep, analyze blood oxygen, even provide ECG functions, as if equipping everyone with a personal physician. But this "digital skin" involves far more than health management; it renegotiates the boundaries between body and the external world, private and public, intuition and quantification. For instance, the fall detection feature on the Apple Watch has saved numerous users' lives by automatically calling emergency contacts and services after sensing a hard fal; professional systems like WHOOP provide athletes with precise training advice and fatigue warnings by monitoring Heart Rate Variability (HRV) and sleep stages. These devices are no longer passive recorders but active participants and guardians, embedded into daily life, becoming part of our biological organism.

However, this "skin" brings not only protection and convenience but also an unprecedented self-perspective and desire for control. We begin adjusting our behavior based on data: going to bed earlier due to a poor sleep score, walking an extra two thousand steps to meet an activity goal, even learning meditation because of a heart rate alert. This seems like practicing the ancient Greek Delphi maxim—"Know thyself"—except now this knowledge is generated by algorithms and presented numerically. But is this also a new form of the "datafied self"? When the body is transformed into a measurable, optimizable object, are we unconsciously narrowing life experience down to calculable metrics? French philosopher Michel Foucault revealed how technologies of power shape the subject through norms, surveillance, and self-examination. In the digital age, this "skin" imperceptibly becomes a tool for self-discipline—we voluntarily wear it, track continuously, and internalize its judgments, understanding health, efficiency, and even happiness as quantifiable and improvable variables.

This layer of "skin" also subtly alters our relationship with our own bodies. Previously, understanding our bodies relied more on internal sensations—fatigue, pain, pleasure were perceived and expressed by ourselves. Now, data is often seen as a more "objective" truth. When a smart band indicates "insufficient deep sleep," even if you feel well-rested, you might doubt yourself; when a fitness app rates today's workout as "average efficiency," even if you felt satisfied, a tinge of frustration may remain. German philosopher Josef Pieper warned in Leisure: The Basis of Culture that when everything is subjected to the logic of efficiency, humans lose the capacity for "non-utilitarian perception". Are we also gradually losing the ability to listen to our body's internal voice, instead relying on external data to tell us "how you feel"?

More importantly, this "digital skin" does not cover everyone equally. It primarily serves those with purchasing power, digital literacy, and health consciousness, thereby imperceptibly widening the health gap. Furthermore, the data models these devices rely on are often built based on specific populations (e.g., young, healthy cohorts in Europe and America), potentially overlooking physiological differences in women, the elderly, people of color, or those with chronic conditions, creating algorithmic bias. While providing protection, this "skin" can also become a tool that excludes heterogeneity and reinforces mainstream standards.

Moreover, as bodily data is continuously uploaded to the cloud, stored, analyzed, and even shared by companies, the body becomes a flowing information node, blurring the boundaries of privacy. Although we voluntarily don this "skin," we can rarely fully know how our data is used, or by whom. The body, this realm that should be most our own, faces unprecedented exposure and risk in its technological externalization.

Yet, we must not overlook the positive potential inherent in this "skin." For chronic disease patients, devices like Continuous Glucose Monitors (CGMs) significantly enhance autonomy; for the elderly, smart devices provide safety monitoring and social connection; for every ordinary person, it can also become a medium for enhancing bodily awareness and promoting self-care.

The true challenge perhaps lies in whether we can utilize technology to enhance the body without losing direct bodily experience; understand ourselves with data without relinquishing awe for life's complexity.

This "digital skin" thus becomes a paradoxical metaphor: it is both a protective film and an exposing layer; a window extending perception and a barrier obscuring intuition; empowering the individual, yet potentially serving hidden powers. It reminds us that the deepest technological revolutions often occur closest to the skin—where human and machine, senses and algorithms, nature and culture quietly intertwine, redefining what constitutes the body and the self.

And we must learn to wear this "skin" without being wholly defined by it; to extend our senses through it, yet not forget the body's authentic, unquantifiable richness and depth.

Section 2: When Technology "Moves In" to the Body

The integration of intelligent technology with the human body is undergoing a profound shift from 'attachment' to 'embedding', moving beyond wearable devices to implantable technology. When technology ceases to be merely a 'digital skin' enveloping the body and truly 'moves in'—in the form of chips, electrodes, and sensors—we face not just a technological upgrade, but a philosophical reconfiguration concerning bodily sovereignty, personal identity, and the very essence of being human.

This is akin to the continuous glucose monitors implanted by some individuals with diabetes; it's no longer just 'worn' on the body, but 'grows' within it, transmitting blood glucose data to a phone in real time. Technology transforms from an external assistant into a permanent internal 'partner'.

This is no longer just tool use, but a blending of technology and life at the physiological level, a co-evolution of code and flesh, an intimacy never before seen in human history, and an unprecedented challenge. We are crossing an invisible boundary, transitioning from beings who use tools into a new form of life that exists in symbiosis with them.

Implantable technology first found application in the field of medical rehabilitation, with the original intent of compensating for functional deficiencies in the human body and restoring damaged physiological capacities. Cochlear implants directly stimulate the auditory nerve with electrode arrays, allowing the deaf to regain the ability to hear the world; retinal implants convert visual signals into electrical impulses, offering the hope of light perception to the blind. These technologies seem to continue the traditional tool logic of 'compensating for defects,' but the method has fundamentally changed: they are no longer external to the body but become part of the nervous system, directly involved in the generation of perception. This is no longer just 'assistance,' but 'replacement' or even 'reconstruction'—technology is not only supporting the body but also redefining what it means to 'hear' and 'see.'

A user who has used a cochlear implant for twenty years shared: "At first, the sounds of the world were like mechanical noise, but gradually, the brain learned to interpret these signals. Now, I can't even tell which sounds come from the technology and which are from memory—they've all become 'my sound.'" This deep integration of technology and sensation marks our entry into a new era: Technology is actively participating in the construction of our perception of the world.

A step further is the development of brain-computer interface (BCI) technology. Companies like Neuralink are exploring the implantation of ultra-fine electrode threads into the cerebral cortex to enable direct communication between the brain and external devices. Paralyzed individuals using such systems can control robotic arms to fetch water, type messages, or even play video games using thought alone. In these scenarios, technology is no longer an extension of the body, but an extension of consciousness; it bypasses damaged neural pathways, rebuilding the bridge between 'intent and action.' This is both liberating and invasive: When a person's intention is no longer realized through muscle contraction and bone movement but through algorithmically decoded neural signals, who is the true agent of the action—the human or the technology? When intention must be 'translated' by an algorithm to take effect, can we still call it pure 'will'? A groundbreaking study from Stanford University illustrated a scenario where a patient paralyzed by a spinal cord injury, using a sensor implanted in the brain, could type text on a computer at 90 characters per minute simply by imagining the act of handwriting. The astonishing aspect of this technology is that it not only decodes brain signals but also learns and adapts to individual neural signatures—technology is becoming a mirror of our nervous system, reflecting and expanding our mental capacities.

All this points to a deeper change: implantable technology is blurring the line between 'tool' and 'body,' thereby unsettling the stability of the 'self.' From a phenomenological perspective, the body is not just an object 'I' possess, but the very way 'I' exist in the world; it is the center of perception, the subject of action, the medium through which the 'self' interacts with the world. When technology is implanted and becomes an indispensable part of perception and action, it ceases to be an object 'I' use and becomes part of 'me.' A person with a cochlear implant doesn't think, 'The device is working,' with every sound heard, but directly experiences 'I am hearing'; a person relying on a BCI to control a robotic arm doesn't feel 'I am operating a machine,' but feels 'I am reaching out.' The technology integrates so deeply into the body schema that it transforms from 'other' into 'self.' This shift is so natural that we often only become aware of its presence when it fails—just as we typically don't notice our own heartbeat unless it falters.

But this fusion also brings new anxieties. On one hand, implants can become a new form of 'disability'—when the system fails, requires an update, or is hacked, the user may instantly lose certain abilities. This dependency is more thorough and potentially more dangerous than ever before. In 2017, the U.S. Food and Drug Administration (FDA) recalled a series of pacemakers due to security risks, as these devices were potentially vulnerable to hacking. This means that the technology which once gave life could also become its point of fragility. On the other hand, the internal logic of technology may inversely shape human cognition and behavior. If a BCI algorithm tends to interpret certain neural patterns as 'intent to purchase' or 'emotional impulse,' could it imperceptibly narrow or even distort a person's genuine will? If memory could be encoded, stored, or even edited, how do we ensure that technology does not tamper with the core experiences that constitute 'who I am'? The Dutch philosopher of technology Peter-Paul Verbeek warned that when technology penetrates the most intimate realms of human existence, it may no longer be just a tool we use, but becomes our mode of being—and this mode may not always align with fundamental human interests.

Furthermore, implantable technology raises profound questions of fairness, access, and ethics. When some can enhance cognition, extend lifespan, and heighten perception through implants, while others lack access to basic healthcare, are we heading towards a new form of biological stratification? When tech companies control the data streams, software updates, and even the on/off switches of implants, could the body become,imperceptibly, a colony of commercial power? These are not futuristic hypotheses but emerging realities. For instance, some experimental implants require regular subscription fees to maintain functionality, otherwise becoming partially or fully disabled—effectively turning fundamental human capacities into rentable commodities. More worryingly, these technologies are often initially accessible only to affluent groups, thereby exacerbating existing social inequalities. We may be entering an era of 'biotechnological stratification,' where some gain significant advantages through technology, while others are excluded from this evolution.

However, we must not overlook the hope and connection this technology can bring. For patients with locked-in syndrome, BCIs may be their only window to the outside world; for those with neurological disorders, implantable stimulation devices can alleviate tremors and pain uncontrollable by medication. Here, technology is not just enhancement, but the provision of basic dignity and the possibility of existence. A Parkinson's patient described the change brought by a deep brain stimulation (DBS) device: "It doesn't make me superhuman; it lets me be 'human' again—able to feed myself, hug my family, and feel the joy of control." These stories remind us that the value of technology is ultimately reflected in how it serves human needs and dignity.

The true challenge lies in whether we can develop technology without losing guardianship over human values; whether we can embrace fusion without abandoning critical reflection. This requires establishing new ethical frameworks and regulatory mechanisms to ensure technological development aligns with the broader human interest. The EU's ongoing development of the Artificial Intelligence Act, which attempts to strictly regulate high-risk AI systems including certain implantable technologies, is an important start, but global cooperation and coordination are still needed.

What does it mean for technology to 'move in' to the body? It may signify humanity entering an ancient dream—transcending the body's limitations, becoming a freer, more capable self. But it also forces us to answer a serious question: When technology and self are so tightly interwoven, how do we defend the foundations of what it means to be human? The answer lies not in the technology itself, but in how we choose to shape it, how we endow it meaning and direction. And this conversation must involve everyone—for this is no longer just about imagining the future, but about the body, mind, and destiny of each one of us.

In this transformation, we are both observers and participants; both users of technology and objects being reshaped by it. Perhaps, in the end, we will discover that the relationship between humans and technology is not opposition, but symbiosis; not replacement, but fusion. In this fusion, we must neither blindly embrace all technological possibilities nor reject progress out of fear. What we need is wise choice, prudent regulation, and deep reflection—

ensuring that technology enhances rather than diminishes our humanity, expands rather than restricts our freedom, and connects rather than isolates our community.

Section 3: Transcending Nature's "Life Programming"

If wearable devices have clad us in a "digital skin," and implantable technology lets machines "move in" to the body, then the deep integration of gene editing, synthetic biology, and artificial intelligence in the life sciences marks our entry into an even more fundamental stage of transformation: humanity is beginning not only to read the language of life but also to rewrite its grammar. This is no longer just about repair and enhancement; it is a reprogramming aimed at the very source of life—we seek to transcend the slow pace of natural evolution, using the hand of technology to redraft the blueprint of "life" itself.

This is exemplified by scientists using CRISPR gene-editing technology to successfully modify immune cells, enabling them to precisely recognize and attack cancer cells, providing patients with specific leukemias with a "living drug." Technology is transforming from a tool that repairs life into a "pen" that writes life's instructions.

The core of this shift lies in humanity's newly acquired ability to directly intervene in the genetic code. Gene-editing technologies like CRISPR-Cas9, acting like precise "molecular scissors," allow scientists to cut out disease-causing variants and insert functional genes. Operations once confined to science fiction are now laboratory reality. For instance, researchers have successfully used gene editing to treat inherited disorders like sickle cell anemia and beta-thalassemia, offering unprecedented hope for a cure. But this is more than a medical advance; it is a philosophical turning point: Life is gradually shifting from a given gift to a designable project. We are crossing an ancient boundary, moving from "understanding nature" to "rewriting nature," even attempting to become nature itself.

Yet, while we cheer this "programming freedom," we must also confront the profound perplexities it brings. If life can be written, who holds the power of the pen? And what ethical grammar should be followed? Gene editing touches not only disease treatment but also the possibility of enhancing human physicality, intelligence, and even emotion. Imagine if future parents could choose their child's height, intelligence, or emotional predispositions. Are we unintentionally narrowing the value of life down to a set of optimizable parameters? The German philosopher Jürgen Habermas warned that once humans become the object of their own design, human autonomy and inviolability face a fundamental threat. We may be approaching a tipping point: no longer "I think, therefore I am," but "I program, therefore I am"—where the basis of existence shifts from being naturally given to being technologically constructed.

Furthermore, "life programming" brings not only ethical dilemmas at the individual level but also deep challenges to social structures and civilizational ideals. When we can intervene in genetic information through technology, the definition of social equity will also be rewritten. If genetic enhancement becomes a privilege available only to some, then inequality will no longer begin with background, education, or opportunity, but will be rooted at the biological level— potentially creating the most insurmountable class division in human history. As a commentary in Nature cautioned, we may be stepping into a "genetic class society."

But technology itself is never a monochromatic monster. In the eyes of families plagued by hereditary diseases, gene editing is not a luxury option but the only beacon of hope. One mother said, "I don't want a 'perfect' child; I just want a child free from suffering." This simple yet poignant statement reminds us that the meaning of technology is ultimately gives by human circumstances and needs. The real challenge is not to halt progress, but to ensure that technological advancement remains tethered to a human scale— how to alleviate unnecessary suffering without extinguishing life's contingency and diversity.

Beyond gene editing, it is just one part of the grand picture of "life programming." Synthetic biology is creating organisms that have never existed in nature, potentially used for energy production, plastic degradation, or drug manufacturing. In 2010, the team of American scientist Craig Venter first synthesized the artificial life "Mycoplasma laboratorium" in a laboratory, its genome completely designed by computer and assembled chemically. This breakthrough not only demonstrates the power of the technology but also compels us to reconsider the definition of "life": If life can be written from scratch, is it still the "nature" we traditionally understood? Although "Mycoplasma laboratorium" is currently confined to controlled laboratory environments and has not entered natural ecosystems, the future release or leakage of such "designed life" could trigger unforeseeable chain reactions. We stand as if before a forest no one has ever entered, holding tools to map it but also carrying the risk of starting a fire.

Culturally, "life programming" is also subtly reshaping our attitudes towards the body, disease, and even death. Traditionally, illness and disability were often seen as a natural part of life to be accepted; now, they are increasingly framed as "repairable technical problems." This shift brings hope but also harbors a danger: Are we losing the capacity to coexist with fragility and reconcile with our limits? The Canadian philosopher Charles Taylor, in Sources of the Self, reminds us that the human pursuit of perfection should not come at the cost of denying human finitude. The value of life resides precisely in its inherent imperfection and uncertainty.

More notably, the current development of life programming technologies is primarily led by a few tech giants and developed nations. For instance, most genetic research is based on data from populations of European ancestry, leading to diagnostic tools and treatments that are less effective for other ethnic groups. This "scientific bias" not only affects medical equity but could also standardize the future criteria for life programming, diminishing the diversity of human genes and cultures.

Indeed, the changes brought by life programming extend far beyond science and technology; they touched our deepest understandings of spirituality, fate, and human meaning. In many traditional cultures, life is viewed as a gift, carrying a certain sacredness or natural mystery; the programming mindset, however, tends to see life as an optimizable, customizable project. The tension between these views is not easily reconciled. One ethicist aptly compared it: "We are like apprentices who have just received the source code, excited but not yet comprehending the system's profundity and complexity." In pursuing technological breakthroughs, perhaps we need a dose of "technological humility" - acknowledging the limits of our understanding, admitting that some boundaries should not be crossed lightly.

Therefore, alongside advancing life programming technologies, we urgently need to construct corresponding ethical frameworks and governance mechanisms. This includes, but is not limited to: establishing global regulatory standards to prevent misuse; promoting public participation in discussions to align technological development with societal values; strengthening long-term tracking studies of technological consequences, especially ecological and intergenerational impacts; and safeguarding the privacy and autonomy of personal genetic information. Technology itself cannot determine its own direction; only human wisdom and values can guide it toward benefit, not ruin.

Ultimately, "life programming" is not merely a technological revolution; it is a cultural, spiritual, and even existential awakening. It forces us to answer: What parts of life are precious? What vulnerabilities and limitations must we preserve? What is the essence of humanity that we should not alter, even if we can?

Perhaps the true breakthrough lies not in how thoroughly we can reprogram life, but in whether we can wield this power with sufficient wisdom and humility—not playing the creator, but becoming guardians of life; not pursuing perfect individuals, but embracing a more just and compassionate world. On this journey to redefine life, we must hold both scientific curiosity and humanistic care; we must bravely write the future, yet often look back at those things technology cannot encode: love, chance, suffering, hope—it is these, precisely, that make us human.

Section 4: The Definition of "Human" Trembles in the Face of Technology

We stand at a decisive tipping point in the evolution of human civilization and technology. Technology is no longer just changing how we live; it is redefining the "human" itself. When AI composes moving poetry, when algorithms understand our desires better than we do, when mechanical limbs convey authentic touch, that once self-evident concept—"what is a human?"—begins to blur.

For instance, when an amputee feels the warmth of a loved one's handshake through a bionic arm and says through tears, "This is me." And when a chatbot provides consistent emotional support, we can't help but wonder: Has it, in some sense, also become a "companion"?

The boundaries of consciousness are dissolving before our eyes. Neuroscience research shows that after a period of using a prosthesis, the brain remaps its neural networks, incorporating these external devices as part of the self. This means our biological boundaries are no longer fixed but expandable and redefinable.

Even more profoundly, the very definition of consciousness is being challenged. When a Google engineer publicly claimed the AI system LaMDA possessed sentience, regardless of whether it was true consciousness, it forced us to contemplate: If a machine can simulate emotional expression so convincingly, should we grant it some form of moral status?

Memory has long been considered a core component of personal identity, yet digital technology is altering this. Brain-computer interface technology is developing methods to record and store memories, theoretically allowing people to relive any past moment in the future. While this sounds utopian, it harbors deep philosophical questions: If memories can be precisely recorded, selectively deleted, or even edited, does identity also become malleable and optional?

Consider this scenario: A patient with post-traumatic stress disorder alleviates their suffering through memory-editing technology. But does this also change their identity? Do the painful experiences that shape us define who we are as much as the joyful ones? The German philosopher [Context indicates a potential paraphrased reference; specific philosopher and quote verification recommended for final publication] warned, "When we begin to optimize memory, we may unintentionally optimize away ourselves." Technology offers liberation but also carries the risk of self-alienation—we could become the editors of our own lives, yet also potential underminers of its authenticity.

Emotion has always been seen as humanity's most essential, irreplicable domain, yet this realm is also being profoundly influenced by technology. Affective computing has developed AI systems capable of recognizing and understanding human emotions, deployed in fields ranging from marketing to mental health. Going a step further, social robots offer friends or partners who will never judge you. But what does this relationship with artificial emotion mean? When algorithms can provide tailored emotional responses, the messy, complex, and unpredictable nature of human relationships seems less appealing. We face a paradox: the better technology simulates emotional connection, the more we may drift away from real human connection—imperfect but genuine.

In an era where algorithmic recommendations determine what we see, buy, and even who we date, human autonomy—our capacity for independent decision-making—is being subtly eroded. This is not just a privacy issue but a direct challenge to human agency—our sense of being autonomous actors. When an algorithm knows my preferences better than I do, when I rely on navigation systems and no longer cultivate my own sense of direction, when writing assistants help me conceive and express, in what sense am I still the author? The philosopher of technology Ivan Illich foresaw this "disabling of capabilities" in the 1970s—tools should enhance human ability, but when they become too powerful, they can render us incapable. We gain convenience but pay a price: the growth gained through struggle and error, the resilience built while finding our way through confusion, the insight achieved by breaking through writing blocks - these experiences that constitute the depth of character are being replaced by smooth efficiency.

Perhaps the most profound challenge comes from anti-aging technologies and digital immortality projects. When Google invests heavily in aging biology, aiming to "cure" death itself, and when digital immortality projects promise future consciousness uploads to the cloud, these endeavors force us to confront a fundamental question: Is death not merely a limit of life but also a source of meaning? An octogenarian expressed it profoundly: "Knowing life is finite makes me cherish every sunrise, forgive minor grievances, and dare to love even though it might hurt. If life were endless, would we still live so intently?" If death were no longer inevitable, would our choices, love, and creation hold the same urgency and value?If consciousness could continue indefinitely in the digital realm, the very concept of "life" would require redefinition.

Amid this fundamental trembling, we are not powerless. Thinkers worldwide are seeking new ways to understand human nature. Perhaps the definition of "human" was never fixed. From the humanist enlightenment of the Renaissance to modern neuroscience's exploration of consciousness, humanity's self-understanding has constantly evolved. The challenges posed by technology do not seek to destroy humanity but invite us to participate in a more conscious process of self-creation. In this process, we may need to return to basic philosophical questions: What makes life worth living? What is the core of being human that we must never trade away? Technology can enhance many human capacities, but can it cultivate wisdom, compassion, and deep connection?

A developer of care robots shared her moment of insight. When the robot she tested performed all care tasks perfectly, yet the patient still felt a sense of "lack," she realized: "They didn't need efficient service, but the feeling of being seen and understood." So she redesigned the system, incorporating more 'inefficient' human interaction elements—occasional imperfect responses, appropriate silences, even intentional "mistakes." As a result, patient satisfaction significantly improved. This simple yet profound story reveals a key insight: While pursuing technological efficiency, we must preserve space for those seemingly "inefficient" yet quintessentially human qualities—vulnerability, uncertainty, spontaneity, and genuine encounter.

As we stand in this moment of definitional tremor, the ultimate question we face is perhaps not 'What will technology turn us into?', but 'What do we want to become?' Technology offers possibilities, but the agency remains in human hands. We need collective wisdom, cross-cultural dialogue, and deep ethical reflection to navigate this unknown territory. Ultimately, the definition of the human may not vanish within technology but could be expanded and deepened through dialogue with it.

In this sense, technology's greatest gift may not be the answers it provides, but the questions it raises; not the solutions it offers, but the reflection it compels. As we collectively confront these profound questions, we are not losing our humanity but participating in its next evolution.

Section 5: The Essential Return to a "Human-Centered" Future Dwelling

Amid the flood of intelligent technology pouring into daily life, we were once deeply fascinated by precise algorithms and seamless interactions, as if the ultimate mission of technology was to endlessly optimize efficiency and convenience. However, as living spaces gradually fill with sensors, data flows, and smart devices, a fundamental question emerges: Is the final goal of technology to create a "perfect" environment requiring no human participation, or to return to the human being itself—serving human needs, emotions, and values? The development of the intelligent dwelling is shifting from a technology-led narrative towards a profound return to being "human-centered."

In the early days of the technology, there was a certain fascination with 'smart' itself. Manufacturers were eager to demonstrate how to control all home appliances by voice, how to achieve automated scene linkages, attempting to reshape the home into an efficiently operating system. But this techno-centric thinking overlooked the most crucial point: the essence of home is a place for people, not a collection of machines. Some families reported having to alter long-standing habits to adapt to the system's "automation"; other users complained that "smart scenes" actually increased operational complexity, making simple things cumbersome. Behind these mismatches lies technology transforming from a tool into a goal, with people reduced to objects adapting to it. As the technology philosopher Lewis Mumford noted, "Over-reliance on technological efficiency can gradually cause humans to lose their sense of control over life itself, becoming appendages to technological logic."

True "human-centered" design first means technology respects diversity and inclusivity. Every household has its own rhythm and composition; there is no one-size-fits-all algorithm. The ideal intelligent system should possess the capacity to learn and adapt, rather than relying on preset controls. The "Adaptive Scenario System" from the domestic smart home brand Aqara is instructive: users can customize rules via a "drag-and-drop" interface—a commuter sets a "Commute Mode" to automatically open curtains and start the coffee machine at 7 AM; someone working from home sets a "Focus Mode" to mute entertainment notifications and dim non-essential lighting at 9 AM. The system also supports "differentiated family member permissions": an elderly mode retains only basic functions like turning lights on/off and adjusting temperature, while a children's mode blocks control of dangerous devices. This design shift signals the industry's move from "what technology can do" back to "what people need," echoing what sociologist Anthony Giddens emphasized: "Good technology should serve as an 'enabling tool,' not a 'disciplinary means,' must provide possibilities for different lifestyles, rather than imposing a single standard."

A deeper layer of being "human-centered" lies in technology's response to emotional and psychological needs. Home is not just a physical container but an emotional anchor. The "Empathy House" launched by Panasonic Japan in 2024 offers a warm answer: using cameras to capture micro-expressions and voice modules to analyze tone, if it detects a couple arguing with heightened emotions, it automatically warms the lighting, plays soothing music, and pops up a suggestion like "Would you like to watch some old family videos?"; if it detects a solitary elder being still and silent for an extended period, it might simulate a grandchild's voice saying "The magnolias downstairs are blooming," and push community activity notifications. These features have nothing to do with efficiency but touch the soft spots of the heart—technology can be more than a problem-solving tool; it can become an emotional companion.

In the current context of an aging population, being "human-centered" is even more evident in the care for specific groups. According to National Bureau of Statistics data, China's population aged 60 and above reached 297 million in 2023. Ensuring the elderly are not "marginalized" by the smart era is a crucial task for intelligent dwellings. The "Age-Friendly Smart Renovation Project" in Shanghai's Yangpu District serves as a strong reference: installing "voice-controlled smart grab bars" for mobility-impaired elders—saying "Turn on the light" both illuminates the room and can trigger a fall alert; designing "tactile switches" with differently shaped buttons for the visually impaired; most critically, all devices retain traditional controls, e.g., smart locks support both fingerprints and mechanical keys, preventing elders from being trapped by system failures.

For people with disabilities, smart technology is a vital support for independent living. The "Barrier-Free Smart System" co-developed by Tencent Cloud and a non-profit organization allows users with high-level spinal cord injuries to control curtains, adjust air conditioning, and send voice messages using only eye-tracking technology. These practices affirm the principle of the UN Convention on the Rights of Persons with Disabilities: "Technology should promote social inclusion and ensure all persons enjoy life's conveniences equally—this is the core of technological ethics."

Cultural adaptability is also key to being "human-centered." Eastern families emphasize multi-generational living, requiring smart homes to balance diverse needs; Western families prioritize personal space, needing technology to find a balance between sharing and privacy. The "Garden-Style Smart Residence" in Suzhou deeply integrates Eastern elements: smart partitions use Suzhou embroidery craftsmanship, able to switch patterns depicting the four seasons; study lighting simulates natural light changes, recreating the garden's "scenery that changes with every step"; during traditional festivals, the large screen automatically plays old family photos and suggests recipes favored by elders. The "Nordic-style Smart Home" jointly launched by Sweden's IKEA and Volvo focuses on the symbiosis of humans and nature: smart windows adjust their opening based on sunlight, rainwater is used for watering plants; the temperature control system prioritizes ventilation over air conditioning, aligning with the local habit of "minimizing AC use."

Today, user attitudes towards technology are also shifting. Initially drawn by novelty, more people now question ethical boundaries: where does the data go? Do algorithms manipulate choices? Can the system be 'paused' at will? This awakening is pushing the industry towards transparent design. In 2024, Xiaomi's "Privacy-Controllable Smart System" adopted a "local storage first" approach, allowing users to choose storage methods and view data records; Huawei's smart speaker added an "algorithm explanation function," stating, for example, "Recommended based on your 30-day folk music play history and today's weather," rather than a vague "based on your preferences." These changes are building a new technological ethic: intelligence should not be an "invisible controller" that subtly permeates, but a clear and visible "considerate assistant." It lets users always maintain the initiative of choice, neither forced to accept preset rules nor kept in the dark about data usage, truly making the "human" the master of technology use.

From a philosophical perspective, the "human-centered"

intelligent dwelling re-examines the relationship between technology and people. Heidegger warned that technology can lead people to view the world through a "calculable" lens, whereas the meaning of home lies precisely in preserving the unquantifiable parts: aimless chats, sudden inspirations, quiet contemplation. One family planned to install a "learning monitoring system" in their child's room; the designer suggested adding a "free exploration mode"—turning off monitoring in the evening, turning on starry sky lights, and playing nature sounds. Follow-up feedback showed that the child's learning efficiency actually improved after having "time to daydream." This illustrates that technology's value lies not in eliminating life's "uncertainties," but in preserving the human right to "enjoy uncertainty."

The future intelligent dwelling will likely move away from the "fully automatic" utopia towards "symbiotic" intelligence: technology handles repetitive tasks and provides safety support, while people focus on creation and emotional connection. This division is not a regression but a sign of technology's maturity—understanding its boundaries and comprehending its purpose of service. As Carl Sagan said in The Demon-Haunted World, "The finest technology is that which you don't even notice is there, but gives you just the right help when you need it."

Ultimately, the direction of the intelligent dwelling depends on our answer to "what is a good life"—which has never been a "perfect process" precisely planned by algorithms, but the "real daily life" where one can breathe freely and place emotions. Technology cannot define happiness for us, but it can help sweep away life's trivial distractions, giving us more energy to embrace each other and preserve memories: it's the light an elder can easily turn on, the starry sky under which a child can daydream freely, the old photos automatically playing when the family gathers around. Making a home intelligent is never about building a museum filled with technology, but nurturing a harbor where one can "feel at ease being oneself"—a place with warmth, memory, and a sense of belonging. We will eventually understand: the smartest home is not the one that best predicts behavior, but the one that best respects human autonomy and embraces human complexity. It does not chase cold efficiency but guards the warmth of lived-in moments; it does not fear life's uncertainties but gives people the courage to explore the unknown.

This is technology's deepest empowerment—not to live life for people, but to help each person become themselves more vividly and completely.

Co-evolution:
A New Species in the Workplace

1. Restructuring Roles: How AI is Redrawing the Map of Work

2. Human-in-the-Loop: The Efficiency Revolution and the Trust Paradox in Collaborative Models

3. The Skills Chasm and Identity Anxiety: Humanity's Survival Dilemma in an Era of Co-evolution

4. The Irreplaceable Human Anchors: The Breakthrough of Creativity, Empathy, and Critical Thinking

5. The New Ethics of the Workplace Ecosystem: Balancing Algorithmic Fairness and Human Agency

Chapter 4
Co-evolution: A New Species in the Workplace

AI's entry into the workplace has long surpassed the simplistic narrative of "machines replacing humans." It is no longer merely an efficiency tool for automating repetitive tasks, but is emerging as a "new species" that is restructuring the workplace's role map, division of labor logic, and collaboration ethics. Our relationship with it has shifted from "using" to "collaborating in feedback loops." Within this seemingly seamless cooperation, however, the value of human skills and identity is quietly being placed on shifting sand. This chapter will dissect the efficiency revolution and survival dilemmas within this co-evolution, and pose the question: As AI becomes an indispensable "partner" in our work, are we harnessing a new productive force, or are we being reshaped by a new production logic? And where should we cast the anchor of that which is irreplaceably human?

Section 1: Restructuring Roles: How AI is Redrawing the Map of Work

When an administrative specialist in an office building discovers that AI can not only automatically generate meeting minutes but also prioritize action items based on the logic of participants' comments; when a veteran factory technician watches a robotic arm precisely execute a welding technique he spent a decade mastering, even adjusting parameters in real-time via sensors to avoid deviations— a widespread assumption is crumbling. We thought AI was just an "efficiency tool," at best replacing some repetitive labor, without realizing it is triggering a reconstruction concerning the very "essence of professional identity."

Public discourse on AI and the workplace has long been trapped within the framework of a "replacement narrative": certain clerical jobs will disappear, junior copywriters will become unemployed, assembly line workers will be replaced... These predictions are not entirely wrong, but they remain superficial. The real impact of AI on the workplace is never just a list of "who will be phased out." Rather, it is dismantling the traditional logic whereby "professional identity = fixed function," pushing humans into a new predicament of "fluid job functions" and "blurring professional identities," ultimately forcing us to re-examine the fundamental question: Is the meaning of work for humans about "completing specific tasks," or about "realizing existential value"?

The root of this questioning lies in a philosophical shift in the relationship between technology and humans. Heidegger, in The Question Concerning Technology, defined traditional technology as an "instrumental framing"—like a blacksmith wielding a hammer, shaping it for a plowshare according to the needs of tilling, or for a nail according to the purpose of fastening; a programmer writing code— if the user needs "quick bill checking," they write the corresponding query logic; if the company needs "data leak prevention," they code protective programs. Ultimately, these technologies are methods to extend human capabilities further: the hammer transmits the blacksmith's "strength" more accurately, code turns the programmer's "ideas" into actionable solutions. From start to finish, humans hold the initiative; how to use the technology and for what purpose is determined by humans. Humans remain the masters of technology, and the "existential dimension" of work is thereby established: the blacksmith confirms their value in "transforming material" through forging, the programmer realizes the meaning of "problem-solving" through coding. Tools are merely the media that amplify this value.

But AI has broken this one-way "human-led, tool-assisted" relationship. It is no longer a "hammer" passively waiting for instructions, but a "collaborator" that can proactively engage in the entire process of "task definition, execution, and optimization."Take the operation position at an internet company as an example. In the past, the functional boundary of "content operation" was clear: planning themes, writing copy, and formatting for publication. Humans led every step, and tools (such as typesetting software) only served to reduce operational costs. Today, AI first recommends "workplace anxiety topics that Gen Z cares more about" based on user profile data, then generates three initial drafts of copy in different styles, and can even predict the open rates of different formats based on past publication data. At this point, the operator's work has shifted from "independently completing content production" to "calibrating AI's recommended direction, optimizing copy details, and judging the rationality of data predictions."In this change, "job functions" are no longer fixed "what to do," but dynamic "what to do together with AI"; humans are no longer "the sole executors of tasks," but "coordinators of human-AI collaboration."

The emergence of this "collaborator" identity is blurring the traditional boundaries of professional roles, and this blurring is breeding a deep-seated identity confusion. Let's take the ancient profession of "accountant" as an example. Before AI's involvement, the accountant's functional chain was complete and clear: from auditing source documents and recording ledger entries to preparing financial statements and filing tax returns, each link relied on professional knowledge and experiential judgment. "Accurate recording and compliant tax filing" was the core label of an accountant's professional identity. A veteran accountant with twenty years of experience once said, "As long as I can get the accounts right and keep the company's taxes in order, I feel I'm a qualified accountant." This certainty of "mastering a complete function" was a key source of professional security. But now, AI financial systems can automatically identify invoice information and enter it into ledgers, provide tax risk warnings through algorithmic comparison, and even generate financial analysis reports based on business data. The accountant's work is fragmented into tasks like "reviewing anomalous data flagged by AI," "adding explanations for special transactions AI couldn't identify," and "interpreting the AI-generated report for management." An accountant undergoing this transition confessed, "Now I spend my day looking at invoices flagged red by AI on my computer. Sometimes I can't find the issue for hours. Once solved, I have to figure out how to translate the AI's 'cold report' into something the boss can understand. I sometimes ask myself, am I still an accountant? If AI can eventually solve anomalies itself, what will I do?"

This confusion is not an isolated case but a widespread condition across industries. In creative fields, a designer's work shifts from "conceiving visuals from scratch" to "adjusting initial designs generated by AI," leading some to joke about becoming "AI photo retouchers." In education, parts of a teacher's lesson preparation are handled by AI—it can generate targeted teaching plans based on students' mistake data, while the teacher spends more time "judging if the plan suits the class's learning situation" and "designing interactive elements AI cannot replace," leaving many teachers feeling their professionalism is being "diluted." In healthcare, AI-assisted diagnostic systems can quickly identify lesions in medical images, shifting the doctor's focus to "reviewing AI diagnosis results" and "formulating treatment plans combined with patient history," causing anxiety among young doctors who wonder, "If I only check the lesions marked by AI, how am I different from a fresh graduate?" This anxiety is essentially a conflict between "functional fragmentation" and "identity integrity." We are accustomed to defining our professional identity by the ability to "independently complete a certain type of integral task," while AI disassembles these tasks into numerous small segments of "human-machine collaboration." When people can no longer confirm their self-worth through integral functions, the foundation of professional identity begins to shake.

More importantly, AI is not only dismantling existing functions but also creating new roles "without precedent," whose "ambiguity" is even greater. The "AI Trainer" is a typical example. On job boards, this role is often described as "optimizing AI model data, tuning algorithm parameters, improving AI output accuracy." But in practice, the job content varies dramatically by industry: an AI trainer in healthcare needs medical knowledge to annotate pathological features in case data for the AI; in customer service, they need understanding of communication psychology to teach the AI to recognize users' latent needs; in education, they need pedagogical logic to optimize the content structure of AI-generated lesson plans. A medical AI trainer said, "My daily tasks are very mixed. I need to look at scans with doctors to mark tiny lesions the AI missed, communicate with algorithm engineers to explain 'how to describe this lesion's features in data,' and sometimes train hospital staff on how to use our AI system. When I describe my job now, it takes a long time to explain. Even my parents don't know if I'm a doctor or a computer person." This "cross-disciplinary, non-standard" role characteristic makes it difficult for practitioners to find the "identity anchor points" that traditional professions offered. In the past, teachers knew their value lay in "educating students," doctors in "healing the sick." But today's AI trainers, human-machine collaboration consultants, and data interpretation specialists struggle to define their core value in one clear sentence. This state of "value suspension" is more disconcerting than "functional replacement."

We must acknowledge that the "replacement narrative" is popular because it offers a "manageable anxiety"—as long as we know which jobs might disappear, we can learn new skills to avoid the risk. But the challenge posed by the "reshaping logic" is precisely its "unmanageable ambiguity": you don't know how your function will be dissected by AI tomorrow, what competencies new roles will require, or how to define your professional identity in the future. Behind this ambiguity lies a fundamental rewriting of the "work-and-human" relationship by technology: in traditional work, humans achieved self-identity through "mastering tools and fulfilling functions"; work was a "means for human existence." In the AI-restructured workplace, work is beginning to become a "process co-defined by humans and technology," where humans must seek existential value within "dynamic collaboration with AI"—this is the most profound aspect of the restructuring of division of labor. It not only redraws the map of workplace roles but also compels us to rethink the ontological question of "why humans work."

We cannot return to a "traditional workplace without AI," nor can we simply accept an "AI-led functiona split." The only way forward is to re-anchor human "irreplaceability" within this restructuring. This irreplaceability will no longer stem from the "ability to complete specific tasks," but from the existential power to "define the meaning of tasks, coordinate human-machine relations, and realize value connections." This, perhaps, is the true revelation offered by the "restructuring of division of labor": the map of workplace roles will change, but the existential value of the human will always remain the core that technology cannot replace.

Section 2: Human-in-the-Loop: The Efficiency Revolution and the Trust Paradox in Collaborative Models

When a radiologist at a top-tier hospital opens an AI-assisted diagnostic system, the lung CT scan on the screen already highlights three suspicious nodules, with the system providing an assessment: "62% probability benign, 38% probability malignant." This is not a simple case of "AI acts first, human checks later," but rather a cyclical flow of "AI generates preliminary conclusions → human reviews and calibrates → data feeds back to iteratively improve the AI"—a process academia terms the "Human-in-the-Loop." This model is driving an efficiency revolution in fields like healthcare, finance, and law: medical AI can reduce average image diagnosis time from 30 minutes to 5 minutes; financial AI triples the efficiency of risk control reviews; judicial AI speeds up document processing by 60%. Yet beneath the halo of efficiency, a deeper ethical and epistemological dilemma is quietly spreading: when we rely on AI to provide the decision-making "scaffolding," reducing ourselves to "calibrators," how can we trust a non-human intelligence that cannot articulate its "thought process"? When the AI's "black box" becomes bound to human "judgment," who bears responsibility—the code, the user, or the developer? The core of this collaborative revolution is not "how to make AI more efficient," but rather "how to safeguard human subjectivity and moral boundaries within this efficiency."

The trust crisis in the human-in-the-loop model stems first from the "inexplicability" of algorithms—this is the predicament of the "black box society" Warned by Shoshana Zuboff in The Age of Surveillance Capitalism. The deep learning models of AI are like sealed black boxes; the logical chain between input data and output results is obscured by vast parameters and complex computations. Even the developers often cannot fully trace the generation process of a specific decision. In a bank's AI credit system, a small business owner with a good credit history might be flagged as "high-risk" and denied a loan. When the owner asks why, the account manager can only give a vague reply: "result of the system's comprehensive assessment." This isn't necessarily evasion; the system itself cannot generate an "understandable explanation." It might have simultaneously considered cash flow volatility, industry policy changes, and even regional economic data. The weighting and interrelation of these factors are encoded into the algorithm but cannot be translated into a human-comprehensible "because A, therefore B" causal logic. This "lack of a right to explanation" directly undermines the foundation of trust: humans cannot trust a collaborative partner that cannot even explain "why it did this," just as we wouldn't let an equivocating doctor write our prescription. Although the EU's GDPR explicitly grants citizens a "right to explanation," requiring companies to provide "clear and comprehensible" explanations for automated decisions, in reality, most firms either refuse to disclose algorithmic details citing "commercial secrets," or provide "explanations" still filled with technical jargon, rendering the right a formality. This contradiction— "rights on paper,predicament in practice"—leaves humans in the loop in an awkward position of "passive calibration." We don't know where the AI went wrong, we can only judge based on experience whether the "result seems reasonable." This calibration feels more like "guesswork" than rational collaboration.

More tricky than the lack of explicability is the ambiguity of responsibility. AI lacks moral agency; it can neither bear legal responsibility nor feel moral remorse. Therefore, the responsibility within the "human-in-the-loop" must ultimately fall on humans. But the question is, when human decisions are strongly influenced by AI, how should the boundaries of responsibility be drawn? In 2022, an accident involving an autonomous vehicle occurred in a city: the AI system misidentified a stationary construction vehicle as a "cloud" and did not trigger braking, while the human driver, having grown reliant on the AI's warning function, failed to react in time, resulting in a collision. After the accident, the manufacturer blamed the "driver for failing to monitor," while the driver argued that "the AI's misjudgment was the primary cause." This case reflects the core ethical contradiction of the human-in-the-loop: when AI becomes the "primary suggester" of decisions, the human's "calibration responsibility" gradually becomes diluted. We subconsciously think "the AI's judgment is more reliable," leading to lowered vigilance, even abandonment of independent thought. This psychology of "responsibility transfer" is particularly dangerous in high-risk domains. In medical scenarios, if a doctor over-relies on AI's diagnostic suggestions, they might overlook subtle anomalies simply because the "AI didn't flag them." In judicial settings, if a judge references an

AI's sentencing suggestion, they might acquiesce even if it seems too harsh, swayed by the "algorithm's basis in massive case data." In these situations, while humans appear to be in the loop of "AI generates options, human reviews and calibrates," they have effectively lost their core stance as the primary decision-maker. We are no longer the "dominant calibrator" who corrects AI bias based on actual circumstances, but have instead become the "endorser" providing formal confirmation for the AI's conclusions. On the surface, medical responsibility still rests with the doctor, but when the AI's "data authority" becomes the implicit basis for decisions, the doctor's independent judgment is compressed, and their actual decision-making power is quietly eroded by the algorithm's "authority."

A deeper predicament lies in the lack of "alterity" in the human-machine relationship, which can be illuminated by Levinas's ethics of the Other. Levinas posits that the "Other" is a being different from the self, possessing an unassimilable quality. Human moral responsibility arises from respect and empathy for this "Other"—it is through face-to-face interaction with the Other that we perceive their unique needs and emotions, thus motivating moral action. But AI is not a true "Other": it has no consciousness, no emotions, and certainly no dimension of "self." Its "responses" to humans are essentially mechanical data processing, not understanding based on empathy. In a psychological counseling platform's model of "AI initial screening + human counselor follow-up," the AI might recommend a counseling direction based on user-inputted "emotion keywords" (like "insomnia," "anxiety"), but it cannot capture the latent emotions behind the user's words—for instance, the tone of exhaustion or perfunctoriness when a user says "I've been sleeping well lately," which a human counselor can detect but the AI cannot. This "lack of empathy" means that "collaboration" within the human-in-the-loop remains at the "functional level," unable to ascend to the "ethical level." AI can provide decision suggestions, but it cannot understand the concrete impact of these suggestions on humans—it doesn't know that denying a loan might plunge a small business owner into crisis, nor that a misdiagnosis could cause a patient to miss a critical treatment window. When we collaborate with AI, we are not facing an "Other who can perceive our situation," but a "tool focused solely on outcomes." This relationship lacks the emotional connection necessary for morality, making genuine trust impossible to build. Levinas's theory reminds us that true collaboration is not just "functional complementarity" but "ethical interaction"—and AI can never become such an "Other," as it lacks the capacity to "see" human uniqueness and vulnerability.

This is not to negate the efficiency value of the human-in-the-loop model, but to recognize soberly that efficiency is merely the "superficial goal" of collaboration; safeguarding human subjectivity and moral responsibility is the "deep foundation." To resolve the trust paradox, we need improvements at the technical level—such as developing "Explainable AI" to make algorithmic decision logic transparent. We also need standard at the institutional level—like establishing "algorithmic audit mechanisms" to clarify responsibility distribution when AI errs. Most crucially, we need an awakening at the conceptual level—we must constantly remember that AI is a "collaborative partner," not a "decision-making authority." The human's calibration responsibility involves not just "checking the result," but also "scrutinizing the AI's logical premises" and "considering the specific human context." Within the human-in-the-loop, genuine trust does not stem from "the AI's accuracy rate," but from "human confidence in their own judgment"—we are not trusting the AI, but trusting "our own ability to judge whether the AI is reliable."

When a radiologist discovers a tiny lesion not flagged by the AI, they are demonstrating the core human value within the loop: not passively accepting the AI's suggestion, but proactively using their own professional knowledge and moral perception to compensate for the technology's limitations. Such actions have little to do with efficiency, but they embody a respect for individual patient differences—it is the warmth of humanity. This judgment and insistence, this commitment to actively steering the direction, not blindly following algorithmic standards, and keeping human needs central when collaborating with technology, is precisely the "light of human subjectivity" we must never relinquish.

Section 3: The Skills Chasm and Identity Anxiety: Humanity's Survival Dilemma in an Era of Co-evolution

Lao Zhou, a senior Java programmer at an internet company, has been staying up late lately, staring blankly at the handwritten code manuscripts from his youth. With 18 years in the industry, he once built his reputation on precise algorithm optimization skills, becoming a core member of his team. But now, after the company introduced AI coding tools, he finds that backend logic which used to take him three days to write can be drafted by AI in half an hour—often with potential bugs automatically avoided. When HR suggested he "focus on learning AI prompt engineering and code review," Lao Zhou agreed verbally, but a hollow feeling churned inside him. His worry wasn't about an inability to learn new skills, but a sudden, deeper doubt: "After all these years as a programmer, was it because I could write code that I became 'Lao Zhou,' or did writing code make me 'Lao Zhou'?"

Lao Zhou's confusion pierces through the superficial appearance of a mere "skills gap." Public discourse often reduces workplace challenges in the age of technology to "obsolete old skills, insufficient new skills," overlooking a more profound truth: what AI is dismantling is not just specific professional competencies, but the very "professional identity" that humans rely on to construct their selfhood—the core vessel that allows us to answer "Who am I?" and "What is my purpose in the world?" As Ulrich Beck argued in Risk Society, the nature of risk in modern society has shifted from "external natural disasters" to "endogenous technological risks." In the workplace, the most fatal technological risk is not the "threat of unemployment," but "identity collapse": when the professional functions that form your livelihood are deconstructed by technology, when the professional narrative you've built over decades is easily rewritten, you plunge into a survival crisis concerning your very "meaning of existence."

The root of this dilemma lies in the logic of constructing self-identity in modernity. Anthony Giddens, in Modernity and Self-Identity, proposed that individuals in modern society no longer define themselves through "lineage" or "family" as in traditional societies, but through a "reflexive project of the self"—we actively choose careers, build life trajectories, and weave our professional experiences into a coherent "self-narrative" to confirm "who I am." For Lao Zhou, being a "programmer" wasn't just a job; it was the central chapter of his self-narrative: from "staying up all night debugging code as a rookie" to "leading the team to overcome technical challenges." These experiences made him believe he was a "technical expert capable of solving complex problems." This identity provided more sustenance for his sense of existential meaning than his salary ever could. The emergence of AI coding tools directly severs the logical chain of this narrative—if the core act of "writing code" can be outsourced to AI, where does the identity of "technical expert" anchor itself? The anxiety caused by this "narrative fracture" cannot be alleviated simply by "learning AI prompts," because it touches not on the question of "whether my skills are useful," but the ontological question of "whether Iam useful."

More cruelly, the accelerating pace of technological iteration is fostering what can be called a "liquid career"—akin to Zygmunt Bauman's "liquid modernity," where all stable structures dissolve. A career is no longer a linear path "from apprentice to master," but a fluid process of "constant fragmentation and reconstruction." Xiao Lin, a marketing specialist at a FMCG company, has had to change her core skill set three times in five years: she started with social media operations, learning content strategy; then the company pushed AI user profiling, forcing her to cram data analysis; this year, the demand is for mastering AI-generated marketing copy and performance optimization. She jokes that she's "like someone perpetually racing to catch the last bus—the moment I catch one, the route changes." Xiao Lin's plight is not unique. A 2024 workplace survey indicates that the "shelf life" of skills for professionals has shortened from 3 years to just 1.5 years, with over 70% of workers reporting that "skills become obsolete before they are even mastered." This state of "perpetual catch-up" creates a dual anxiety: the pressure of "unending learning" on one hand, and the confused of an "unstable identity" on the other. The moment you define yourself as a "data-driven marketer," technology demands you become an "AI-collaborative marketer." Your self-narrative remains perpetually "unfinished," unable to find a stable anchor for your value.

Beck's "risk society" theory also highlights that a key feature of modern risk is "individualization." In traditional societies, professional risks were shared by the collective (e.g., everyone faced unemployment during an industry downturn). Now, technological risk is decomposed into an individual responsibility ("If you can't learn new skills, it's your own problem"). This "shift of responsibility" makes the anxiety harder to bear. Technology frames career predicament as a matter of "individual capability," ignoring objective constraints like age, access to learning resources, and cognitive habits. This leaves individuals not only facing "obsolescence" but also burdened with the moral pressure of "not trying hard enough."

We must acknowledge that technological change never presents a purely economic problem; it is a profound ontological crisis. When work can no longer provide a stable identity, when a career can no longer construct a coherent self-narrative, how is humanity to confirm its place in the world? When Lao Zhou stares at his old code manuscripts, what he misses is not just the "self who could write code," but the "self who could prove his value through code." When Xiao Lin races after the latest skill trend, her anxiety isn't just about "failing to learn new skills," but about "never finding her own professional coordinates." These dilemmas cannot be solved by "skill training" alone—because the need is not for "supplementing new skills," but for "rebuilding the foundation of self-identity." This involves, for example, the search for meaning in asking "Is what I do truly useful?", the desire for connection in forming warm relationships with those around us, and the creative impulse to make something new. These yearnings, hidden in every person's heart, can also support our understanding of "who we are," without being confined solely to the box of "what job I do."

Of course, this rebuilding is inevitably difficult. Just as Lao Zhou, when trying to shift from "writing code" to "guiding AI to write better code," still feels a sense of loss when looking at his youthful code. Just as Xiao Lin, after mastering AI marketing tools, still reminisces about "the days of writing hit copy based on intuition." But perhaps, this state of "moving forward with a sense of loss" is the new normal for human existence in the technological age. We need not demand that we immediately find new identity coordinates. Instead, through "constant adjustment and continuous reflection," we can gradually construct a self-identity that is not dependent on any specific skill. After all, the meaning of human existence has never been solely about "what one can do," but fundamentally about "the choices we make about who to become"—and this, no matter how technology evolves, will never change.

Section 4: The Irreplaceable Human Anchors: The Breakthrough of Creativity, Empathy, and Critical Thinking

When AI can write logically rigorous reports, create aesthetically pleasing designs, and even generate rhythmic poetry, people inevitably ask: What remains for humanity that technology cannot replicate? The answer lies not in the "complexity" of skills, but in the "existential" qualities of being human—those capacities rooted in our perception of the world, our care for others, and our responsibility for the future, abilities that cannot be decomposed into data and parameters by algorithms. Hannah Arendt, in The Human Condition, distinguished between "labor," "work," and "action": labor is repetitive activity for survival, work is the production of artifacts, and "action" is the uncertain practice betweenpeople that can initiate new possibilities. This philosophical distinction illuminates the essence of three core human capacities: critical thinking is the "practical wisdom" for navigating complex situations; empathy is the "foundation for action" in building ethical relationships; creativity is the "courage to act" in breaking existing frameworks. They are not cold items on a "skill checklist," but the fundamental way we, as living beings, reach out and interact with the world—the very roots that allow us to stand firm amidst the waves of algorithms in the technological age, and not lose ourselves.

The irreplaceability of critical thinking stems from its role as a fundamental human capacity for confronting "complexity and uncertainty."This ability involves not just "analyzing data," but the reflective practice of "questioning premises, weighing values, and accepting consequences"—precisely where AI is weakest. AI's logic for problem-solving is "input data → match model → output result." It relies on known rules and historical data but cannot question the "rationality of the rules themselves." In a corporate downsizing decision, an AI model based on "performance data + labor costs" might recommend laying off senior employees with "long tenure, high salaries, but recently average performance." From an algorithmic logic perspective, this is the optimal solution for "cost optimization." However, a human decision-maker, employing critical thinking, might ask: "Could the average performance be because these senior employees are undertaking more 'mentoring and training'—

91

an intangible contribution? Would cutting them sever the team's chain of experience?" This leads to adjusting the plan, retaining the senior employees, and redesigning the performance evaluation system to include intangible contributions. The key point is not that the AI's calculation is inaccurate, but that it cannot, like a human, "step outside the model to see the problem"—it cannot perceive the human situation behind the data, weigh the value conflict between "efficiency" and "fairness," nor bear the long-term ethical consequences of the decision. Hans Jonas, in The Imperative of Responsibility, emphasized that humans in the technological age need "forward-looking responsibility," meaning being accountable for the future impact of their actions. This sense of responsibility is at the core of critical thinking: we must not only judge if the "result is correct," but also reflect on whether the "goal is legitimate" and the "process is just." AI has no concept of "responsibility"; its "judgment" always serves a pre-set goal, never questioning the value of the goal itself. When a financial AI recommends pushing high-interest loans to low-income groups, or when a judicial AI tends to recommend harsher sentences for specific demographics based on historical data, it is human critical thinking that "calibrates" the direction of the technology. This tolerance for "complexity," this weighing of "values," and this acceptance of "responsibility" constitute a "practical wisdom" in action that algorithms can never replicate.

The irreplaceability of empathy lies in its role as the cornerstone for constructing human ethical relationships.This capacity is not the technical operation of "recognizing emotions," but an existential connection involving "perceiving the Other and responding to the Other." As Emmanuel Levinas argued, "ethics begins with the responsibility for the Other," and empathy is the starting point of this responsibility. AI can recognize that a "user is in an anxious state" through vocal tone and facial expressions, but it cannot truly "understand" the specific situation behind the anxiety: it knows the client is feeling down when they say "I'm worried the project will fail," but it doesn't know if this anxiety stems from a commitment to the team, responsibility for family, or concern for their professional reputation—these unique life experiences hidden behind language represent an "existential blind spot" that AI cannot penetrate. In hospice care scenarios, AI can play soothing music and remind caregivers of procedures, but it cannot, like a human caregiver, hold the elderly person's frail hand, sensing their fear of death and nostalgia for the past in the silence; it can say "Don't be sad," but it cannot, like a human, touch the softest corner of the person's heart with a phrase like "I know you miss your children." The "action" Arendt spoke of is essentially about "people illuminating each other." Empathy is the medium for this "illumination": it allows us to transcend the boundaries of the "self," see the uniqueness and vulnerability of the Other, and thus make a warm response. Cases from a psychological counseling platform show that when facing users with "suicidal tendencies," AI can mechanically list a "helpline," whereas a human counselor might first share a tiny personal experience of "having been in a low place," using the empathy of "I understand this difficulty" to break the user's sense of isolation. This interaction of "setting aside judgment and embracing vulnerability" is not a program an algorithm can simulate; it is the instinctive response of humans as "ethical beings." When technology tries to replicate empathy with "emotion recognition models," it just happened to ignore the essence of empathy: it's not about "knowing the Other's emotion," but about "sharing the burden of the emotion with the Other." Within this burden lies the entire weight of human ethical relationships.

The irreplaceability of creativity is ultimately manifested as humanity's existential expression of "transcending algorithmic logic and opening new possibilities." This creation is not the technical operation of "recombining existing data," but an "action that breaks through," imbued with moral imagination and capable of pointing toward new values. AI's "creativity" is essentially "imitation and splicing": it can generate new lines of poetry based on the rhythms of millions of poems, but it cannot, like a human poet, infuse words with personal life trauma and reflections on the era to create "new meaning" that touches the soul; it can generate new artworks based on the compositions of millions of paintings, but it cannot, like a human painter, leave an "irreplicable imprint of life" on the canvas, born from a unique perception of the world. The reason Arendt's "action" can "initiate new possibilities" is precisely because it is full of human "contingency and uniqueness"—creativity is the ultimate embodiment of this "action": it is not the optimization of existing rules, but the establishment of new rules; not the recombination of the known, but the summoning of the unknown. Jonas's "moral imagination" is particularly crucial here: human creation is never "aimless revelry," but an attempt to add new value to the world, carrying responsibility for the future and care for others. In an educational project for "left-behind children" designed by a public welfare organization, AI can provide "personalized learning plans," but it cannot, like a human designer, conceive the idea of "having left-behind children paint their hometowns, then using AI to animate the paintings to share with their parents." The core of this idea is not technical cleverness, but a deep insight into the emotional need of "left-behind children missing their parents" and a creative safeguarding of the value of "family connection." While AI can assist with the "technical aspects" of design, what ultimately determines the value of creativity remains the human reflection on "what people need" and "what the world needs." This creativity, imbued with moral warmth and directed toward new meaning, represents a "courage to act" that algorithms can never attain.

The common core of these three capacities is humanity's "capacity for response"—response to complex situations, response to the needs of the Other, response to future possibilities. AI can only "execute" preset commands, while humans can "respond" to undefined problems; AI can only "conform" to existing models, while humans can "break through" the boundaries of models; AI can only "serve" given goals, while humans can "question" the meaning of goals. In the technologically driven co-evolution, we need not fear AI surpassing humans in "efficiency." What we truly need to safeguard is the human warmth inherent in our capacity to respond to the world and to others. As Jonas said, "The faster technology develops, the more we need to slow down and think about what kind of people we want to become." And these three irreplaceable human anchors are precisely our foundation for answering this question: the value of humanity lies never in being "more efficient than technology," but in existing in this world "with more warmth, more depth, and more courage than technology."

Section 5: The New Ethics of the Workplace Ecosystem: Balancing Algorithmic Fairness and Human Agency

When Xiao Li, a delivery rider for a food delivery platform, stares at the constantly ticking "delivery countdown" on his phone and runs a red light in a downpour; when Xiao Zhang, an operations specialist at an internet company, is forced to abandon substantive content creation in favor of crafting clickbait headlines to meet an AI-defined "user dwell time KPI," we are witnessing far more than a simple story of "technology enhancing efficiency." We are seeing algorithms, as a new form of power, reshape the ecological rules and power structures of the workplace. The "data extraction and behavior modification" Shoshana Zuboff exposed in The Age of Surveillance Capitalismhas deeply penetrated the workplace: AI monitors employees' labor processes in real-time (riders' locations, customer service call durations, programmers' lines of code), decomposing complex labor into quantifiable, optimizable metrics, and then uses algorithmic commands to discipline employee behavior in reverse. Behind this "algorithmic management of everything" lurk three hidden dangers: power is consolidated in the hands of the corporation, leaving no room for employee input; fairness is fragmented by algorithms, consistently disadvantaging suburban riders and female job applicants; and humans are gradually reduced to "cogs" within the algorithm, forgetting what they truly want to achieve. Solving this predicament isn't about rejecting technology outright, but about establishing new rules for the workplace—auditing algorithms like we audit finances, prioritizing "human well-being" in design, and creating rules collectively, ensuring technology truly serves as a tool for people, rather than managing them.

The imbalance of power under algorithmic governance is the primary challenge for the new workplace ethics.In traditional workplaces, while power between employees and employers was unequal, a space for negotiation still existed. In the algorithm-dominated workplace, power achieves an invisible yet absolute concentration through "data and code": the corporation holds the rights to design the algorithm, interpret the data, and modify the rules, while employees cannot even get a clear explanation for "why the KPI was suddenly raised" or "why my performance score is lower than my colleague's." A customer service team at an e-commerce platform faced this dilemma: their AI suddenly compressed the standard for "single call duration" from 5 minutes to 3 minutes, while demanding a "98% customer satisfaction rate." The service agents were forced to quickly interrupt customers' requests while anxiously trying to soothe their emotions, with many facing pay cuts for failing to meet the targets. When they asked their supervisor for the "basis of the standard," the only answer was the vague reply: "the algorithm adjusts automatically based on business needs." This is the power game hidden within the algorithmic "black box": the corporate desire to "do more with less" is embedded into the algorithm and packaged as an "objective scoring standard," without allowing employees to understand "why I scored low" or "if it can be changed." Worse, algorithms use "data labels" to stratify people: a recruitment AI, based on historical data showing "female employees leave faster," secretly deducts points from female candidates; a performance AI, focusing on superficial data that "suburban riders are slower," labels Lao Chen as "inefficient," causing him to earn significantly less than urban riders. These cases prove that the lack of algorithmic fairness is never merely a "technical bug," but an extension of power structures in the data age: when algorithms are controlled by a few and lack external oversight, they inevitably serve the interests of the controllers, not the fairness and well-being of all employees.

The erosion of human agency is a deeper crisis of algorithmic governance.It not only "takes over" tasks and dictates how they are done but also gradually grinds away the very sense of "why we work." Hannah Arendt, in The Human Condition, emphasized that the value of "work" lies not only in the output but also in the "self-expression" and "interaction with the world" that humans achieve through labor. Algorithms, by reducing labor to a mechanical process of "meeting metrics," strip away this meaning. Xiao Wang, a copywriter at an advertising agency, once said: "Before, when I wrote copy, I would ponder the brand's tone and the user's real needs. Even after ten revisions, it felt valuable. Now the AI generates three drafts first, and I just need to tweak the wording to meet the 'readership target.' Sometimes I look at what I've written and wonder what meaning it even has." Behind this "loss of meaning" lies the gradual ceding of human agency: when algorithms define the standard of "good work" (like KPIs, data metrics), and when employees must have their value confirmed by algorithmic scores, we lose the autonomous judgment of "what work should be"—it's no longer "I want to do something valuable," but "the algorithm wants me to do something that meets the target." More seriously, algorithms subtly alter employees' cognition through "behavioral shaping": to avoid overtime, riders gradually accept "running red lights as normal"; to shorten call times, service agents gradually ignore "the customer's real appeal"; to meet "code submission speed," programmers gradually sacrifice "code readability and security." This process of twisting one's own work habits to keep up with the algorithm's rhythm is, in essence, a process of slowly losing one's own mind—we no longer demand of ourselves according to "human standards," but discipline ourselves according to "algorithmic standards," ultimately becoming "appendages" of technological logic.

Building a new ethics for the workplace ecosystem requires a concerted effort across "technological, institutional, and social" dimensions, with the core aim of rebuilding "human agency" and the "servant role of algorithms."

At the technological level, promoting "explainable and auditable algorithm design" is foundational. This means algorithms can no longer be treated as corporate "trade secrets" but must be subject to oversight by third-party audit bodies (comprising technical experts, ethicists, and employee representatives). The audit should cover not only the fairness of the algorithm but also its reasonableness. One tech company has piloted an "algorithm audit system": each quarter, a third-party team reviews the AI performance system. If they find that "the KPI achievement rate in a certain department is below 30%," the company is required to reassess the algorithmic logic. This led to a 15% reduction in that department's "daily active user indicator" and the inclusion of "user retention quality" in the assessment. Such auditing isn't about "rejecting technology" but about returning technology to its "tool attribute"—ensuring algorithmic goals align with human capacity and ethical bottom lines.

At the institutional level, establishing "multi-stakeholder algorithmic consultation mechanisms" is crucial, transforming employees from "passive recipients of algorithms" to "participatory co-designers of algorithms." This can draw on the principle in the EU's AI Act that "high-risk AI systems must solicit the views of stakeholders." Companies should be required to invite employee representatives to participate in need definition and rule-setting when designing workplace AI (e.g., for recruitment, performance, risk control). A manufacturing enterprise, when introducing an AI production scheduling system, organized a consultation group of "engineers + frontline workers." The workers pointed out that "the AI ignored equipment maintenance intervals," leading the engineers to optimize the algorithm by adding "equipment maintenance buffer periods," ultimately balancing production efficiency with reduced overtime for workers. The value of this consultation mechanism lies in breaking the monopoly of "unilateral rule-setting by the corporation," allowing algorithms to truly reflect "human needs," not just serve "capital's interests."

At the social level, reshaping a "human-centric view of technology" is fundamental. This requires moving beyond the "efficiency-first" technological narrative and rethinking the relationship between "technology and humanity." The ultimate goal of technology is not to "replace humans" or "control humans," but to "enhance human capabilities" and "improve human well-being." This means corporations can no longer use "cost reduction and efficiency gains" as the sole criterion for introducing AI; they must also consider "employee career development" and "the sense of meaning in work." Society can no longer equate "technological progress" solely with "economic growth"; it must als follow technology's impact on "human dignity." One internet company, when introducing AI content assistance tools, did not use them as "tools to replace copywriters," but as "tools to liberate copywriters' creativity"—the AI handles "basic information integration," while the copywriters focus on "deep creativity and emotional expression," supplemented by a "creative reward fund" encouraging warm, substantive content. The core of this approach is making technology serve "human creativity," not the other way around.

The new ethics of the workplace ecosystem is not about "restricting technological development"—it's not about forbidding the use of AI to optimize customer service management, but about ensuring that technological development does not deviate from the track of humanity. It demands that when we discuss "algorithmic efficiency," we simultaneously question "algorithmic fairness"; when we discuss "data-driven" approaches, we simultaneously follow "data privacy respect"; when we discuss "human-machine collaboration," we simultaneously safeguard "human agency." When delivery riders no longer have to risk danger to escape an algorithmic countdown, when customer service agents no longer have to ignore clients to shorten call times, when copywriters no longer have to abandon creativity to cater to data metrics—thenhuman-machine collaboration becomes truly ethical and warm; thenthe workplace ecosystem truly serves human dignity and development.

Ultimately, this discussion about "algorithmic fairness and human agency" is essentially a response to the question of "how should humans exist in the intelligent revolution?" As Hans Jonas stated in The Imperative of Responsibility, "Humans in the technological age need to treat technology with greater prudence and responsibility." This responsibility lies not only in developing more advanced algorithms but also in ensuring that algorithms consistently serve ultimate human values: freedom, dignity, and happiness. This is the core of the new workplace ethics, and the foundation for preserving our humanity in the midst of co-evolution.

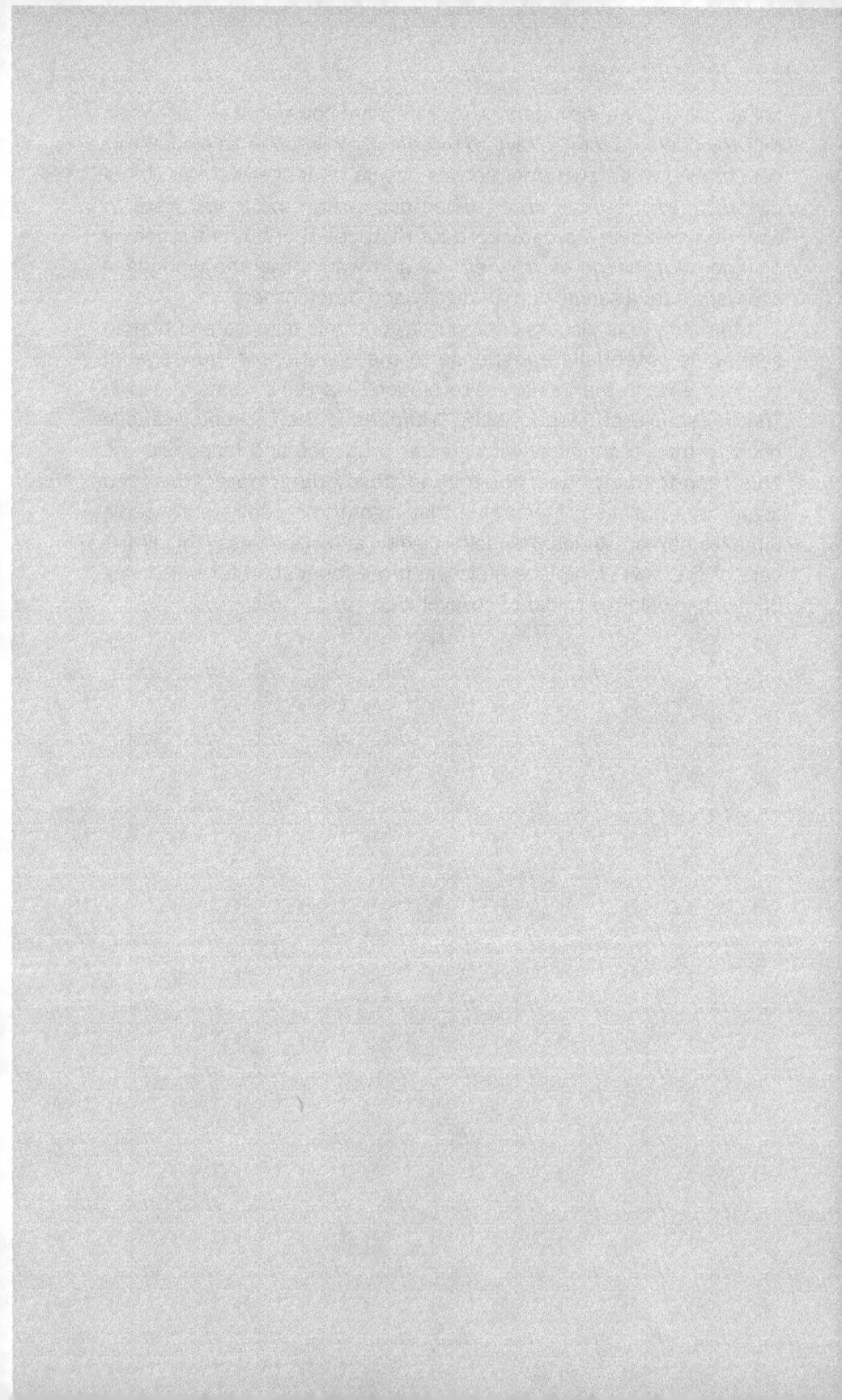

The Urban Brain:
The Pulse of a Living Organism

1. The Transformation of Data Visualization: Making the City's Perception Visible and Tangible

2. When Urban Space Becomes a "Conversational Interface"

3. The Ethical Boundaries of Public Aesthetics

4. Letting the Smart City Grow a "Human Touch"

Chapter 5
The Urban Brain: The Pulse of a Living Organism

The city, humanity's most complex creation, is being endowed with an unprecedented "capacity for perception" by billions of sensors and algorithms. It is as if it has acquired its own nervous system, capable of sensing the pulse of traffic flows, the breath of crowds, and the metabolism of energy in real-time. Data visualization makes the city's rhythms visible and tangible, while intelligent interfaces allow space to become something we can converse with. This chapter will explore the operational logic of this "living organism" and examine the shadows cast by its brilliance: when the urban brain optimizes everything in the name of efficiency, are we building a smarter, warmer home, or are we constructing a precise framework that standardizes and makes predictable human behavior? Ultimately, whose well-being should the city's "intelligence" serve?

Section 1: The Transformation of Data Visualization: Making the City's Perception Visible and Tangible

At 6 p.m. in Hangzhou's Qianjiang New City, the LED light bands along the riverside promenade change their intensity and color with the flow of traffic: when the average speed on the Qiushi Elevated Road drops below 20 kilometers per hour, the lights shift from a translucent light blue to a somber reddish-brown; when the Desheng Expressway clears up, the light bands ripple with a coherent aqua-green wave, like a breeze blowing across a lake. Citizens out for a stroll don't need to look down at the "congestion index" in their navigation apps; a glance at the flowing colors on the river's surface instinctively tells them "now is not a good time to take the elevated road." This kind of urban perception, which bypasses rational analysis and acts directly on the senses, is the magic of data visualization. It is no longer the traditional transmission of information via "charts + numbers," but a revolutionary "technical embodiment" of urban perception: by transforming abstract data captured by millions of sensors into colors, rhythms, and movements perceivable by the body, it reshapes the emotional connection and cognitive mode between citizens and the city. From a phenomenological perspective, this is a reconstruction of the "structure of urban perception"; from the perspective of media theory, it is both a contemporary practice of McLuhan's "extension of the senses" and carries the risk of sensory isolation warned of by Virilio's "dromology"—we are relearning "how to see the city" through visualization.

Data visualization is, first and foremost, a concrete application of McLuhan's theory of "sensory extension" to urban life. Our eyes naturally cannot see abstract data like "passenger flow distribution," but a visualization screen transforms this data into a heatmap we can directly perceive, like giving our eyes "X-ray vision," helping us sense the city's operational state which we normally cannot touch. In traditional cognition, human perception of the city is limited to the "range physically accessible to the body": we can see the congestion in front of us, but not the traffic flow three kilometers away; we can feel the lighting in our own building's hallway, but not the energy consumption of the entire community. Data visualization acts as a "sensory amplifier," integrating and transforming data from sensors scattered throughout the city's corners, ultimately extending it into a "visual sense that can cover the entire city."

The "City Light" interactive screen on Shanghai's Bund is a typical example: it transforms real-time traffic data from 120 roads in Huangpu District into flowing "light streams" on the large screen—dense light streams represent traffic congestion, sparse ones indicate free-flowing roads. Tourists standing across the river don't need to know specific traffic volume numbers; just by observing the density of the light streams, they can instantly grasp the traffic situation of the entire area. This extension is not simply "seeing farther," but transforming "abstract data" that humans cannot directly perceive into "concrete symbols" that conform to visual perception habits. Just as McLuhan said, "the medium is the extension of man," data visualization is precisely the "extension of urban perceptual capacity"—it turns citizens from "local perceivers" into "global perceivers," breaking the physical limitations the body imposes on urban cognition.

However, phenomenology teaches us that true perception is

not just "seeing," but also "bodily involvement." The deeper value of data visualization lies in constructing a new "structure of urban perception," turning data from an "object of rational analysis" into an "experience perceptible to the body." Heidegger proposed the "intertwining of Dasein and the world," emphasizing that human cognition of the world is not a subject's observation of an object, but an interaction between the body and the environment. Data visualization achieves precisely this kind of "intertwining": it transforms data into elements perceivable by vision, touch, and even hearing, allowing citizens to "unconsciously" perceive the city in their daily activities. For example, Tokyo's Shibuya "Crossing Data Pillar": this 5-meter-high pillar-like installation adjusts the frequency of its light flashes in real-time according to pedestrian flow at the intersection—fast flashing for heavy flow, slow for light flow, accompanied by slight vibrations (more pronounced with heavier flow). As pedestrians pass by, whether they see the lights with their eyes or feel the pillar's vibrations with their hands, they can perceive the crowdedness of the intersection through their bodies. This perception does not rely on data interpretation but acts directly on the senses as "embodied cognition." Here, data is no longer cold numbers on a screen but is transformed into "the rhythm of light" and "the frequency of vibration," integrated into the daily experience of citizens, becoming part of urban perception.

Yet, Paul Virilio's "dromology" reminds us that the core characteristic of the modern city is "speed"—the speed of data generation, information flow, and urban operation have all far exceeded the capacity of traditional perception. Data visualization appears to be a response to "speed": real-time updated visual symbols allow citizens to keep up with the city's dynamic changes. But this "rapid perception" can also breed new problems—"sensory isolation" and "cognitive shortcuts." Virilio argued that the technological pursuit of speed gradually deprives humans of the perception of "depth," reducing the world to a "spectacle of surfaces." Data visualization is exactly like this: when we rely on the brightness and darkness of LED light bands to judge traffic, we may overlook vehicles stranded due to an accident or elderly people anxiously waiting to cross the street—these "non-datafied" urban details are precisely the embodiment of the city's warmth. A commercial district in Beijing once introduced a "pedestrian flow heatmap visualization screen," using red areas to mark crowded spots and green for sparse areas. Some citizens reported, "Now when I go to the commercial district, I just look at the screen for green areas, but I almost missed my usual café because it was marked green due to low foot traffic." This reliance on visual symbols makes citizens lose the "in-depth exploration" of urban space, focusing only on the superficial "data landscape," creating a sensory "isolation": isolating the real people and real scenes behind the data.

Beyond the risks of AI data errors and system failures that are directly visible, there is a more insidious risk—the mental simplification brought by "cognitive shortcuts." To facilitate quick understanding, data visualization often compresses complex urban data into single visual symbols: red = congestion, green = smooth flow, orange = high energy consumption, blue = low energy consumption. This simplification is a cognitive "shortcut," but it also screens out the complexity behind the data. For example, a city's "commute visualization screen" uses red to mark congested road sections. Citizens see red and detour, but they don't know the cause of the congestion—it could be temporary construction or a traffic accident, and the duration of congestion differs greatly depending on the cause. This "seeing only the result, not asking the cause" cognition leaves citizens' understanding of the city at the level of "surface symbols," losing a deeper understanding of the city's operational logic. More seriously, when data visualization becomes the only channel of perception, citizens gradually lose their capacity for "autonomous observation": previously, they would judge congestion by observing the traffic flow at an intersection; now, they only look at the big screen. Previously, they would gauge a neighborhood's vibrancy by feeling its lighting; now, they only look at the pedestrian heatmap. This "cognitive dependence" alienates data visualization from a "sensory extension" into a "sensory substitute," ironically weakening the direct perceptual abilities humans originally possessed for the city.

So, how can we make data visualization truly serve "human perception," rather than replace it? The key lies in returning to a balance between "embodiment" and "complexity"—good visualization design should integrate data into bodily perception while preserving the richness behind the data. Copenhagen's "City Pulse Installation" is a model: installed in a community central square, it transforms the community's energy consumption, air quality, and public activity data into touchable "light and temperature." Residents place their hands on the installation's glass panel; the panel's temperature changes according to energy consumption levels (warmer for high consumption, cooler for low), while light patterns on the panel flow according to air quality (gentle for good air, hurried for poor). This design achieves both embodied perception of data (feeling temperature, observing light patterns) and conveys the complexity of the data through the combination of "temperature + light patterns" (the relationship between energy consumption and air quality). More importantly, a small explanatory sign next to the installation explains the "relationship between temperature and energy consumption," guiding residents to think about "why is energy consumption high today?" and avoiding the simplification of cognitive shortcuts.

Ultimately, the ultimate goal of data visualization is not to create "flashy urban spectacles," but to build an "emotional connection between citizens and the city"—allowing citizens, through a perceptible visual language, to feel the city's "breath" and "pulse," thereby feeling closer to and understanding better the place they live. When the LED light bands in Hangzhou's Qianjiang New City change with the traffic flow, what citizens feel is not just the traffic condition, but that "the city is flowing with me"; when Shenzhen's smart energy consumption pathway changes color with energy use, what residents feel is not just energy data, but "my shared responsibility for energy with the city." This emotional connection is the core value of data visualization as "technical embodiment."

Of course, we must remain vigilant: data visualization is only "one way" to perceive the city, not the "only way." It can extend our senses, but it cannot replace measuring the streets with our footsteps, observing pedestrians with our eyes, or listening to the sounds of the city with our ears. Only by allowing data visualization and direct bodily perception to complement each other can we both keep up with the city's speed and retain our perception of the city's warmth— this is the true "transformative" power of data visualization: making the city's pulse something that can be seen, touched, and felt with the heart.

Section 2: When Urban Space Becomes a "Conversational Interface"

In front of the grey brick walls of Beijing's Nanluoguxiang, a tourist raises their phone towards a weathered lintel. An AR interface instantly overlays the scene from the 1930s: a woman in a cheongsam emerges from the doorway, the old locust tree at the corner still has its youthful branches, and one can even hear the bell of a rickshaw in the distance. This kind of interaction, which feels like "touching history with a finger," transforms urban space from a silent backdrop into a "conversational interface" capable of responding to human needs—from smart traffic lights adjusting their timing based on pedestrian gestures, to government service terminals answering residents' queries through voice interaction, to community screens recognizing citizens' hand gestures to switch information modules. Technology is reconstructing the city into a "real-time responsive interactive system."

However, the philosophy of interfaces and the politics of space reminder us that beneath the phenomenon of "conversability" lie encoded power and ethical contestation. The interaction design of urban interfaces is never a neutral technical practice: it subtly defines "who can participate in the urban dialogue"—is it the youth familiar with touchscreen operations, or groups who can adapt to diverse modes of interaction? It limits "what can be discussed"—is it information serving commercial needs, or demands covering daily livelihoods? It determines "in what manner the dialogue occurs"— is it reliant on visual interaction, or does it accommodate multiple sensory channels like auditory and tactile? These design choices essentially reshape the power relations of urban space: groups whose needs are prioritized in design gain more interactive voice in urban space, while groups whose needs are overlooked are unknowingly excluded from the urban dialogue system. Donna Haraway's theory of "situated knowledges" reveals that behind all "objective" interactions lurk the perspectives and interests of specific groups; while Michel Foucault's concept of "heterotopia" further points out that the city is inherently a "field of differences" where diverse groups coexist. When the interface becomes the medium for dialogue, those unable to adapt to its rules fall into a "silent predicament." We need to ask: when urban space becomes an interface, does this "dialogue" achieve spatial democracy, or does it reinforce new power inequalities? Is interaction design mediating social differences, or is it becoming a "collaborator" with the power structure?

The "conversability" of urban interfaces is first built upon preset technical rules—behind this seemingly free interaction lies a logic where technical rules, often prioritizing commercial interests, subtly guide user behavior in specific directions; it's not truly "talk about whatever you want." The "smart crosswalk" in Shanghai's Lujiazui once sparked debate: when pedestrians step onto the crosswalk, LED lights on the ground illuminate with their steps, while a voice device near the traffic light prompts "Please cross quickly." If a pedestrian lingers too long, the LED lights flash red and the voice changes to "For your safety, do not linger." This design appears to "respect pedestrian will," but actually confines the pedestrian's "dialogue" to the single goal of "crossing quickly" through dual light and voice prompts—it overlooks that elderly people with slower mobility might need more time, nor does it consider parents pushing strollers needing a more calm and unhurried pace.

From the perspective of spatial politics, this interface design is essentially the "spatial encoding of power": the rule-makers of the interface embed their governance objectives into what seems like "friendly interaction logic," allowing users to unconsciously accept the disciplining of spatial behavior through power in the course of smooth operations. Foucault analyzed the power mechanism of the "panopticon"—achieving self-discipline among the managed through visible surveillance. Urban interfaces upgrade this "visible discipline" into "interactive discipline": it doesn't mandatory directly, but guides user behavior through design, allowing power to permeation into daily life under the guise of "dialogue."

More hidden encoding is hidden in "cultural interactions" like AR guided tours. The AR guide system at Nanjing's Confucius Temple can explain the history of buildings along the Qinhuai River to tourists, but its narrative almost entirely revolves around "literati, ink artists, and imperial southern tours," while saying nothing about the labor of trackers along the river during the Ming and Qing dynasties or the lives of ordinary merchants during the Republic of China era. Haraway's "situated knowledges" points out that there is no "perspective-free knowledge." The "historical dialogue" presented by the AR guide is merely a "mainstream narrative" co-constructed by technical elites and cultural authorities—it simplifies diverse urban memories into singular cultural symbols, allowing tourists to accept filtered knowledge under the illusion of "dialoguing with history." Those excluded marginal narratives, like the silent figures in Foucault's "heterotopias," exist in the city's history but cannot make their voices heard through the interface.

The "conversability" of urban interfaces is always constrained by the user's "technical adaptation ability." While young people use mobile AR to interact with historical buildings, elderly people living alone might not even find the power button on a community smart terminal. While office workers book government services via voice assistants, the hearing impaired cannot understand the interface's voice prompt. This disparity in "the right to dialogue" is essentially the digital divide materialized in urban space—not an abstract "technology gap," but the button an elderly person cannot find, the prompt a visually impaired person cannot hear. If interaction design deliberately ignores these differences—for example, terminals only have touchscreens without physical buttons, or guide screens only consider visual interaction without audio functions—then such design ceases to be a "service tool" and instead becomes a "collaborator" in reinforcing inequality, making life easier for those who can use technology and harder for those who cannot.

Foucault's "heterotopia" theory emphasizes that the value of the city lies in accommodating "difference," not eliminating it. However, most current urban interface designs take the "young, digitally literate, able-bodied" group as the default user, treating other groups' needs as "special cases." An AR navigation system in a Beijing subway station can provide 3D route guidance for sighted passengers but lacks tactile feedback or audio guidance designed for the visually impaired. A "smart shopping guide interface" in a Hangzhou commercial district supports gesture control and voice interaction but does not consider that people with physical disabilities might not be able to perform complex gestures, nor does it offer sign language recognition. These design "blind spots"Essentially negate the "heterotopian" nature of the city—the city is a place where diverse groups like the elderly, youth, people with mobility challenges, and the visually impaired coexist, yet the design focuses solely on the needs of "young people familiar with touchscreens," simplifying the varied demands of different people into a single user habit. In the end, these interfaces fail to become "bridges connecting everyone" and instead become "tools of exclusion": the elderly cannot use the fitness equipment, the visually impaired cannot check the guides, left only to watch others use them smoothly while they themselves are barred from urban interaction.

The "dialogue" of urban interfaces involves not only behavioral interaction but also knowledge transmission. Yet Haraway's "situated knowledges"Reminder us that all information presented by an interface is a "selective presentation" within a specific context, not objective truth. When an AR guide tells a tourist, "This alley was once a gathering place for scholars," it hides the lives of commoners who lived there concurrently. When a community screen displays "This community's employment rate is 90%," it does not clarify whether this data includes gig workers and the elderly. When a smart traffic system prompt "80% probability of congestion on this road section," it doesn't explain whether the congestion is due to temporary construction or a traffic accident—this "selective dialogue" makes the urban interface a medium for "narrative monopoly."

A typical case is an "AR restoration" project in an ancient city: the tech team used algorithms to restore the city wall's "original appearance." Tourists scanning the ruins with their phones could see the complete wall and gate tower. But this "restoration" was based entirely on the "officially recorded" style of the wall from ancient documents, ignoring the shops built by commoners around the wall during the Ming and Qing dynasties, or the defensive fortifications added during the Republic of China era to resist war—these "non-official" historical traces, though real existing in urban memory, were filtered out by the interface for not fitting the "orthodox narrative." Local elderly residents once commented: "I bought candy from a small shop at the foot of the wall when I was a child. That shop isn't in the AR. This isn't our ancient city."

The risk of this narrative monopoly lies in simplifying the city's diverse memory into a single "authorized version," causing users to gradually lose their critical understanding of history while "dialoguing with the city." When interfaces only present "approved" information, and interaction only allows "encouraged" behaviors, this "dialogue" degenerates into a "one-way instill" of power—it appears to respond to user needs but actually shapes user cognition, dissolving the plurality of urban space through technological logic.

Truly ethical urban interface design should not be a tool for encoding power but a mediator of "heterotopias"—it needs to acknowledge the differences among urban groups, allowing diverse needs to find channels for dialogue. The core of this "mediating design" is to incorporate the plurality of "situated knowledges" into the interaction logic, making the interface an "inclusive medium for difference" rather than a "barrier excluding difference."

The key to "mediating design" lies in truly decentralizing the "narrative power" of the interface—not allowing designers or managers alone to decide "what the interface says and how," but enabling diverse groups like the elderly, people with disabilities, and parents with young children to participate in constructing the dialogue content. Amsterdam's "Community Memory AR" project adopts this approach: the tech team does not preset the historical narrative but invites elderly community members, new immigrants, and teenagers to record their memories of the community, then links these stories to corresponding spatial locations. When a tourist scans a particular building, they can simultaneously see an elder's story about "a shelter during WWII," a new immigrant's share of "their first landing spot in the Netherlands," and a teenager's recording of "their after-school secret base"—the interface is no longer a transmitter of a single narrative but a "dialogic platform" for diverse memories, where each group can find its voice in urban space.

When urban space becomes a "conversational interface," what we should truly pursue is not the dazzle of technical interaction, but the equality of spatial power. The ultimate goal of interface design is to ensure the city's "dialogue" is not limited to the technically adept, so that elderly people with limited mobility can dialogue with the community through physical buttons, the hearing impaired can dialogue with traffic through visual signals, and culturally marginalized groups can transmit their memories through the interface. As Haraway said, "The value of situated knowledges lies in diverse connection." The value of urban interfaces also lies herein—it is not meant to eliminate urban heterogeneity but, through design, to enable different groups to achieve truly equal dialogue with the city and with each other within this "heterotopia."

After all, a city that can converse should not only respond to the needs of a few; a warm interface should not leave any group in silence. When AR guides can simultaneously tell the stories of trackers and literati, when smart terminals can adapt to the operating habits of both the elderly and the young, when traffic interfaces can cater to the safety of both able-bodied and disabled people— only then will the urban interface truly achieve the interaction ethics of "people-oriented," making "dialogue" a bond connecting diverse groups, rather than a tool of power.

Section 3: The Ethical Boundaries of Public Aesthetics

On a quiet morning along Suzhou's Pingjiang Road, tourists are often drawn to several lantern-like installations at the lane entrance. Warm yellow light spills through wooden grilles onto the bluestone pavement, blending seamlessly with the surrounding white walls and black tiles. Few notice that the "wick" at the top of the lantern is actually a micro-camera, and that hidden within the grille seams are pedestrian flow sensors. This design, which integrates technological equipment into traditional aesthetics, epitomizes the smart city's attempt to balance "functional requirements" with "privacy protection." As the urban brain requires data captured by millions of cameras and sensors to function, the design of public space is no longer just about "beautification"—it has become a "humanistic buffer zone" between technology and humanity: it must meet the functional needs of urban governance while using aesthetic means to soften the "sense of surveillance" inherent in technology, safeguarding citizens' perception of privacy and psychological security. However, this balancing act is far more complex than it seems: Can biomimetic designs truly eliminate surveillance anxiety? Can gentle prompts avoid becoming excuses for "privacy compromise"? How should information layering define the boundary of "over-exposure"? The ethical boundary of public aesthetics is essentially a tug-of-war between "technology needing to function" and "people needing dignity"—choices like opting for concealed designs, using prompt text, or employing gentle forms, these seemingly minor design details quietly define the "sense of security" and "degree of freedom" in public spaces of the intelligent era. They determine whether citizens feel "covertly watched" or "respected"; whether they feel constrained or able to move freely within the space—all hinge on these detailed choices.

The Aesthetic Camouflage of Surveillance and the Boundary of "Concealment"Surveillance equipment in cities was once a symbol of "cold power"—black bullet cameras and abrupt metal sensors always made citizens feel the oppression of "being watched" in public spaces. The emergence of biomimetic design is an attempt to dissolve this oppression through aesthetics: it disguises technological equipment as natural elements or cultural symbols, transforming it from a "surveillance tool" into "part of the landscape," maintaining visual harmony and psychological comfort in public space while fulfilling data collection functions.

The "Bamboo Node Streetlamp" in Hangzhou's West Lake Scenic Area is a prime example. Traditional pedestrian monitoring equipment is usually a standalone metal box, clashing with the area's natural ambiance. The "Bamboo Node Streetlamp" embeds the monitoring module inside a lamp post designed to resemble a bamboo stalk; the photovoltaic panel at the top is shaped like bamboo leaves, and it even adjusts the light's color temperature with the seasons (warm green in spring, orange-yellow in autumn). Tourists strolling by the lake simply see it as a landscape lamp fitting the scenic area's character, hardly aware of its monitoring function. Staff surveys showed that after installing these lamps, tourist disgust towards "being monitored" decreased by 62%, while the accuracy of pedestrian data collection remained above 95%. The cleverness of this design lies not in denying the necessity of surveillance, but in "softening" the presence of technology through aesthetics— when equipment no longer presents a "vigilant posture" but exists in a "form blended into the environment," citizens' privacy anxiety naturally eases.

Yet the ethical boundaries of biomimetic design also emerge here: How should we grasp the "degree" of disguise? If the design is too concealed, could it become "deceptive surveillance"? A community in Beijing once disguised facial recognition cameras as "bird ornaments" and installed them at the entrances of residential buildings. Residents had their facial data collected without their knowledge, sparking intense controversy.

This controversy reveals that the core of biomimetic design should not be "hiding surveillance," but "reducing a sense of intrusion." It can make devices less obtrusive, but it cannot allow devices to be completely "invisible" to the point where citizens are unaware of their existence. Truly ethical biomimetic design must strike a balance between "integrating with the landscape" and "providing appropriate reminders." For example, tiny text reading "environmental monitoring device" could be marked at the base of "bamboo joint streetlights," and faint data collection logos printed on the back of "phoenix leaf sensors." This kind of design—"neither damaging aesthetics nor concealing existence"—is a respect for citizens' right to know, and also the inherent bottom line of public aesthetics.

When the urban brain needs to collect citizens' data, how can prompt language clearly convey "data usage" without triggering citizens' resistance? This tests the ability of "visual communication" in public aesthetics.Blunt written warnings only intensify privacy anxiety, while gentle visual language can convey necessary information and make citizens feel respected—thus increasing their willingness to cooperate with data collection.

A community in Shenzhen transformed its property management system's privacy agreement interface: it replaced the dense, small-print clause with an illustrated flowchart. Green checkmarks indicated "Data used only for security purposes," yellow exclamation marks indicated "Data will be deleted after 30 days," and a prominent "Agree/Disagree" toggle switch was provided at the bottom. This approach of "transforming complex privacy terms into visual trust signals"—using green for safety, illustrations to lower the comprehension barrier, and optional toggles to grant choice—allows citizens to authorize data based on "clarity and voluntariness." Operational data showed that this gentle prompt design increased user agreement reading rates from 12% to 58%, and complaints dropped by 70%.

However, gentle prompts also carry ethical risks: if "gentle" turns into "vague," could it mislead citizens? A city once installed "smart guide screens" in its metro system, using the prompt "Tap to get routes, start a great journey" instead of "Tapping agrees to collect location data," leading many citizens to unknowingly have their real-time location collected. This kind of prompt that "highlights convenience while hiding key information" is a form of evasion that quietly infringes on citizens' right to know. Gentle visual language should not be an excuse for "withholding information," but a tool for "clear communication." Truly ethical prompt design must adhere to the principles of "transparency and accuracy": essential Information must not be omitted, clear boundaries must not be blurred. No matter how gentle the visual language, the core privacy terms must be clearly visible and easy to understand.

The Layered Display of Information and the Bottom Line of "Respect"Data collected by the urban brain is ultimately displayed to citizens via smart screens in public spaces to achieve "transparency in urban governance." However, if this display is unfiltered, it can easily over-expose individual data, sparking privacy disputes—for example, a community screen directly showing "A certain resident has not paid property fees," or a traffic screen exposing "the face photo of a jaywalker." These displaysseemingly for "public warning," actually violate individual privacy and dignity. The design of layered information display uses public aesthetics to create a buffer between "information disclosure" and "privacy protection": it categorizes display levels based on the "public nature" and "sensitivity" of the data, ensuring disclosed information serves the public interest without leaking private individual information.

A "Smart Community Bulletin Board" in Shanghai provides a good example: it displays community energy consumption data not as specific household usage, but uses a "building-level" heat map—darker colors indicate higher energy use in a building, lighter colors indicate lower use, without revealing unit or household details. For waste sorting data, it shows the "community's overall sorting accuracy rate" instead of naming individual households with poor sorting. This layered display achieves the goal of "public supervision" while protecting "individual privacy."

The key ethical consideration for layered display lies in the rationality of the "classification criteria"—determining which data belongs to the "public domain" and which constitutes "individual privacy" requires joint establishment based on legal regulations and citizen willingness. A city once displayed "foot traffic rankings for certain brand stores" on a large screen in a commercial district without informing merchants that the data source was consumer phone locations, causing merchant dissatisfaction. This indicates that classification standards cannot be unilaterally decided by technical or management parties; they should involve citizen representatives, legal experts, and privacy protection organizations in discussions to ensure that the display of information at each level complies with the "principle of minimum necessity"—i.e., disclosing only the minimal information necessary to achieve public interest, without additional leaking any individual privacy.

Conclusion: The Core of Public Aesthetics is "Warm Presence"The ethical boundary of public aesthetics is, ultimately, drawn around "people"—it's not about how advanced the technology is or how refined the design is, but whether it can accommodate the real feelings and needs of ordinary people. We don't need "invisible surveillance," nor "cold, blunt prompts," nor "bottomless information exposure." What we need is aesthetic design that allows technology to exist with "warm presence"—making surveillance equipment as natural as trees by the roadside, privacy prompts as gentle as a friend's reminder, and information displays as respectful as a community notice. When public aesthetics truly becomes a "buffer between technology and humanity," the public spaces of smart cities can operate efficiently yet be filled with humanistic care; be safe and orderly yet also free and comfortable—this is the ethical pursuit public aesthetics should have in the intelligent era, and the warmth the urban brain, as a "living entity," ought to possess.

Section 4: Letting the Smart City Grow a "Human Touch"

What should a smart city look like? The goal is not to pursue flashy technological spectacle, but to meticulously deconstruct "human needs"—considering the declining eyesight and memory habits of the elderly, the unique perceptions and expressions of people with disabilities, and the innate curiosity and cognitive limits of children, all integrated into interface design. When the city's "brain" weaves a data network from millions of sensors, artistic design acts as the crucial "translator": it transforms the 0s and 1s of code into dialect speech an elderly person can understand; converts on-screen 3D routes into raised tactile paths a visually impaired person can trace with their fingertips; and turns abstract air quality data into changes in light and animal sounds a child can perceive. As Donna Haraway noted, "situated knowledges are always closer to the truth than universal claims." The "warmth" of a smart city lies precisely in the folds of these specific situations—in the voice commands Grandma Zhang can easily follow, in the smart tactile paths underfoot that interact with AR navigation for the visually impaired, in the leaf-shaped lights that illuminate when a child touches them.

Senior-Friendly Interfaces: Weaving Life Experience into Technological Logic Elderly individuals living alone in cities often find themselves shut out of the "conversation" by smart interfaces. It's not that they reject technology itself, but rather the silent interfaces built on "young people's logic"—icons too small, text too dense, operational steps too complex. Facing such an interface is like confronting a door without a handle: they know the services they need are behind it, but they simply cannot open it.

This reveals the core logic of designing interfaces for the elderly: for them, an interface's success at being "conversational" is never about the sophistication of the technology—not the touchscreen's sensitivity or its loading speed. It hinges on whether the design can connect with the trajectory of their past lives, evoking familiar symbols and scenarios sedimented in their memory. In the smart terminal in Grandma Zhang's community, the "Schedule Vaccination" button features a drawing of a pigeon wearing a nurse's cap—a common symbol in hospitals from her youth. The "Contact Community Worker" icon shows the silhouette of a person with

118

a satchel, strongly reminiscent of the neighborhood committee members who once walked the streets. These familiar visual symbols are more effective than any user manual. Seniors don't see alien technological elements on the interface, but rather people and objects encountered over a lifetime. This "situational resonance" is what allows them to set aside their fear of technology.

However, "silent corners" remain behind the interface. A smart terminal designed for seniors in one community supported voice interaction but couldn't understand local dialect terms. When an elderly person said they "needed a master to fix a water leak," the system only replied "Service not found," because its database only contained the standard term "water pipe repair." Other terminals had voice prompts that played too quickly, automatically switching pages before the user could comprehend them; or intrusive ads would pop up during operation, and a mistaken tap would leave the user unable to return to the original screen. These instances of "silence" ultimately stem from designers failing to fully consider the life context of the elderly: they see the "eyesight problem" but miss the "language habits"; they recognize the "operational ability" but overlook the "psychological pace." A truly warm interface shouldn't only solve the "visible" problems but must also listen to the "unspoken" needs. A terminal in a Beijing community, for instance, added a "voice replay + synchronized subtitles" function specifically for those with hearing loss, allowing users to pause and replay at will, with subtitles switchable to a "Senior KaiTi font" where even punctuation marks are enlarged.

Accessible Interaction: Translating the "Visible" into the "Perceivable"The dilemma faced by the visually impaired in smart cities starkly highlights the gap between "visibility" and "perceptibility." While sighted people enjoy 3D route guidance on AR interfaces, the physical tactile paths relied upon by the visually impaired are often blocked by shared bikes or construction barriers. A survey in Nanjing's Qinhuai District found 80% of tactile paths had "break points," and the corresponding AR navigation system, while it could announce "tactile path ahead," could not warn that the path was "obstructed," leaving users caught between a "conversational" interface and a "silent" reality.

The breakthrough came with a multi-sensory interactive design combining touch and sound. On a pilot stretch of road in Nanjing, the raised patterns on the tactile path were given grammatical meaning: dots indicate straight ahead, long bars signal an upcoming turn, and crisscross patterns warn of an obstacle. This is synchronized in real-time with audio descriptions via a phone's AR navigation: "Tactile path changes to long bars in 10 meters, prepare to turn left"; "Crisscross pattern in 3 meters, shared bike on your right." Thoughtfully, ambient sound cues were added—"Can you hear the market vendors? You are 20 meters from the community market"—using sound to build a rich spatial awareness, creating what Foucault termed a "heterotopia." In this space, the visually impaired can perceive the same "route details" as sighted people through touch and hearing, no longer silenced by exclusion from the interface.

Yet, this "conversability" has its limits. Designers might see the general need that "people with disabilities require assistance," but miss the "differences and silences" within the disabled community itself—the dialect sign language used by the hearing impaired, the height requirements of wheelchair users, the simplified expressions needed for those with intellectual disabilities. These "invisible" needs are the true measure of an interface's warmth. A smart directory screen in a Hangzhou community, for example, supports not only standard sign language but also can switch to the local Hangzhou sign language; it offers not just voice prompts but also has a tactile vibration button at the bottom. A wheelchair user can press it to receive a printed route guide. This kind of design, which "sees the silenced," constitutes a genuine respect for the "heterotopia."

Child-Friendly Interfaces: Cognitive Resonance Through Play. Children are naturally disconnected from traditional data visualization interfaces. An air quality monitoring screen in a community square displaying PM2.5 levels as bar charts was utterly ignored by children. But when designers transformed it into an "interactive cartoon tree"—touching the trunk makes the leaves change color based on real-time air quality (green with birdsong, yellow with a squirrel animation, red with a "Time to wear a mask!" hand-drawn bubble—children immediately gathered around to touch, observe, and discuss.

The success lies in reconstructing the interaction using a "child's language." Children may not grasp abstract data like "PM2.5 levels," but they instinctively understand "leaf color" and "animal sounds"; they shun formulaic operations but eagerly engage through touching, imitating, and exploring. A smart sign outside a Chengdu primary school uses animal footprint patterns instead of arrows and guides route choices with a "Forest Concert" story, turning navigation into an adventure. The depth of child-friendly design, however, is tested by its inclusivity. The interface at a special education school in Shanghai supports three interaction modes—touch, eye-tracking control, and voice commands. The flashing light frequency can be adjusted to a low rate comfortable for autistic children, and children with physical limitations can trigger functions via sensors on their wheelchair armrests. This multi-layered design confirms the true essence of a smart city: warmth resides not in technological sophistication, but in the detailed response to each unique life.

Conclusion: A Poetic Dwelling with Technology.Martin Heidegger's concept of "poetic dwelling" finds a new interpretation in the age of smart cities. When traffic lights automatically extend the green time for seniors, when guidance systems maintain tactile channels for the visually impaired, when health terminals are so intuitive that elders forget the complex steps and only remember the reassurance of checking their blood pressure—then technology truly achieves humanization. It ceases to be a cold system and becomes a gentle presence woven into the fabric of life; it no longer pursues maximum efficiency but safeguards human fragility, difference, and poetry.

This is what a smart city should be: not an "efficiency machine" driven solely by data and algorithms, but a "home" where people can breathe easily, converse freely, and dwell poetically. The mission of design here is to ensure technology always maintains a posture of "bending down to meet people"—bending down to listen to the silent needs, bending down to adapt to the overlooked existences, ultimately allowing everyone living in the city to feel the vitality of being "seen, respected, and treated with tenderness."

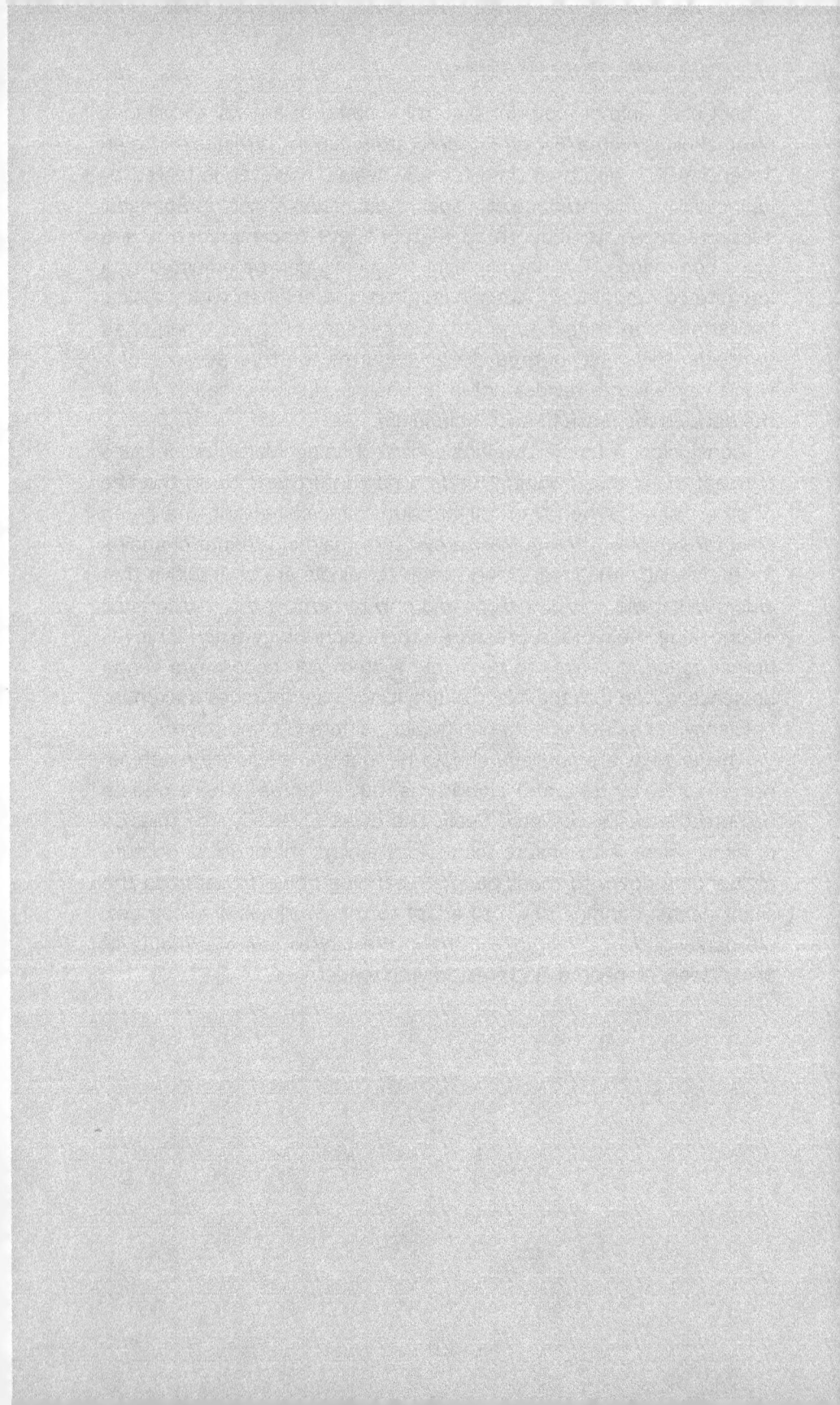

Digital Connection:
The Metaverse of Social Interaction

1. From Interfaces to Encounters: The Rise and Evolution of Virtual Social Interaction

2. The Emotional Paradox of Hyper-Connectivity

3. The Metamorphosis of Self Between Virtual and Real

4. Ethical Dilemmas in the Digital Age

Chapter 6
Digital Connection: The Metaverse of Social Interaction

We stand at an unprecedented crossroads. Technology is no longer just an external tool—it has insinuated itself into our most private sphere: interpersonal relationships. Digital connection weaves an invisible yet omnipresent web, drawing us into a social matrix that is both real and virtual. This space is filled with allure and contradictions: never have we been so close, yet never so lonely; we are free to create identities, yet struggle to define "who I am"; we crave deep connections, yet often get trapped in superficial interactions. This chapter delves into this social metaverse, starting from technological phenomena and moving through cultural, social, and philosophical layers to pose a fundamental question: In the digital age, are human connections expanding toward a broader "sea of stars," or are we falling into more elaborate "isolated islands"?

Section 1: From Interfaces to Encounters: The Rise and Evolution of Virtual Social Interaction

Humanity's desire for connection is an ancient echo etched in our genes. From fables around campfires to letters at post stations, we have never stopped crossing the barriers of time and space to find one another. Yet it was not until the arrival of the digital age that this search unfolded on an unprecedented scale and in unprecedented forms. Our encounters with "the Other" are undergoing a profound evolution—from cold "interfaces" to lifelike "encounters." This is not merely an upgrade in communication methods, but a grand social experiment about existence, identity, and relationships.

The origins of virtual social interaction can be traced back to cold "interfaces." Early email lists, BBS forums, and instant messaging software focused on a core function: "information transmission." The screen acted as a window; through text and symbols typed on a keyboard, we engaged in a strictly coded, delayed form of interaction. Back then, online socializing was like a dance with chains—while it broke geographical limits, it sacrificed the richness and warmth of communication.

The true turning point came with the rise of Social Networking Services (SNS). Innovations such as Facebook's News Feed, Twitter's follow mechanism, and WeChat Moments wove isolated personal pages into a vast, dynamic network of relationships. Social platforms evolved beyond simple "tools" to become "digital environments" or "ecosystems" in which we immerse ourselves. Here, we do more than transmit information—we continuously share updates, curate our images, maintain relationships, and engage in public discussions. Our lives have been "mediated" like never before.

The philosophical significance of this shift lies in its validation of media theorist Marshall McLuhan's assertion: the medium is the message. The form of social media itself—its like buttons, infinite scroll designs, and algorithmic recommendation mechanisms—shapes our behaviors and perceptions more profoundly than the specific content we post on it. It quietly alters how we perceive the world, define ourselves, and build relationships with others.

If social networks are two-dimensional planes, then Virtual Reality (VR), Augmented Reality (AR), and highly gamified social platforms (such as Fortnite and Genshin Impact) aim to build a three-dimensional, "embodiable" social universe. The evolution of technology targets the most core and hardest-to-digitize aspect of human communication: embodiment. In Zoom meetings, we remain "talking heads" (talking avatars) separated by screens. But on VR social platforms like VRChat or Horizon Worlds, we have a controllable "digital body (avatar)." We can nod, wave, dance, and even "high-five" others. While this remains a digital simulation, it introduces a critical dimension to online interaction for the first time: body language.

This experience of "virtual co-presence" holds revolutionary potential. In 2020, American pop singer Travis Scott hosted a virtual concert in Fortnite, drawing over 12 million players who attended as their avatars. They did more than watch the performance—they jumped and danced to the music, cheering alongside thousands of other avatars. This was no longer "watching" a show, but "participating in" and "experiencing" a collective ritual. It blurred the line between audience and performer, creating a shared, immersive collective memory. The shift from "text-based interaction" to "virtual co-presence" is, in essence, a deep simulation of what "encounter" truly is. A real encounter is not just about exchanging information, but about whole-person interaction in a specific space. Technology is trying to replicate spatial awareness, physical interaction, and shared experiences, helping us move closer to the feeling of "truly being together" in the digital world.

Yet this evolution from interfaces to encounters is accompanied by a profound paradox: the more expressive freedom we gain, the more our true selves seem to fade into obscurity. The concept of "hyperreality" proposed by French philosopher Jean Baudrillard feels particularly incisive here. He argued that in postmodern society, symbols no longer refer to reality, but instead self-referentially construct a simulacrum more "real" than reality itself. Social networks are the perfect arena for this "hyperreality."

We carefully curate nine-grid photos for Moments, select Spotify playlists that best showcase our "taste," and share perfectly framed photos of breakfast and scenery on Weibo. Every post is a micro-narrative performance—we are both director and lead actor, collectively building a digital brand called "me." This "me" is not entirely false, but it is usually a polished, one-sided, and strategically presented "best version" of ourselves. Over time, this performance internalizes into a new form of reality. Sociologist Erving Goffman's "dramaturgical theory" finds its ultimate expression here: the world is a stage, and social networks provide the most dazzling lights and the widest audience. Unconsciously, we live according to the script of our "persona," even beginning to confuse our online performance with our offline self. A blogger on Weibo who has gained a large following with an "optimistic and positive" persona may privately be struggling with depression and anxiety—but she dares not break this persona, for "real vulnerability" could destroy the carefully built digital asset she has created.

Thus, the connotation of "encounter" has undergone a subtle shift. What we encounter is more often the personas we are willing to present to each other, rather than our complete, contradictory real selves. Technology provides a grand stage for encounters, yet it also makes us wear more elaborate masks.

Does this mean, then, that "encounters" in the digital age are doomed to be superficial and inauthentic? The answer is not so absolute. Technology amplifies the contradictions of human

126

nature, but it also unlocks new possibilities. For many groups who feel marginalized in real society, virtual social interaction is a form of redemption. Gaming communities offer autistic teenagers a safe, structured space to practice social skills; LGBTQ+ youth gain the courage to embrace their identities by connecting with peers in anonymous communities; enthusiasts of niche cultures can transcend geographical distances to find their "imagined communities." In these scenarios, digital masks are not obstacles—they become armor that protects our true selves and allows us to explore freely.

The crux of the issue may not lie in technology itself, but in how we use it. German philosopher Martin Buber distinguished between two types of relationships in I and Thou: the "I-It" relationship and the "I-Thou" relationship. In an "I-It" relationship, others are objects of our experience and utilization; in an "I-Thou" relationship, by contrast, there is a genuine "encounter" that engages the whole self and sets aside preconceptions. The challenge of virtual social interaction is its tendency to slip into the "I-It" dynamic. We see others as likes, follower counts, or consumable images. Algorithms then push us into "filter bubbles," showing us only what we want to see and further eroding opportunities for genuine encounters with the heterogeneous "Other."

Thus, the evolution from interfaces to encounters ultimately becomes a test of human nature. Technology can simulate all external forms of an encounter—space, body, voice, even facial expressions—but it cannot automatically generate the most core elements of an encounter: sincere openness, the willingness to take risks, and wholehearted attention. A genuine "encounter" may occur when we let go of our obsession with perfect personas and dare to reveal a part of our vulnerability; when we take the initiative to step beyond algorithmic curation and listen to different voices; and when we are willing to invest the same sincerity and patience as we would in offline interactions, even through a screen.

The rise of virtual social interaction has given us an unprecedented breadth of connection. Its evolution, however, forces us to answer an ancient yet profound question: After stripping away all the embellishments of technological media, do we still possess the willingness and ability to truly encounter another soul? The destination of this journey that began with interfaces is not the ultimate simulation of technology, but the return and elevation of humanity's age-old desire for connection.

Section 2: The Emotional Paradox of Hyper-Connectivity

We live in an unprecedented era: with a simple tap on the screen, we can facetime someone on the other side of the globe; post an update and receive hundreds of likes and comments in an instant; join countless group chats, each buzzing with discussions on different topics. We are wrapped in a vast web woven from optical fibers and radio waves—theoretically, more "connected" than any generation in human history. Yet beneath this bustling digital landscape, a new form of loneliness is quietly spreading: a desolation of being surrounded by crowds, an emptiness where every sound can be heard yet none truly reaches the heart.

This is the deepest emotional paradox of the hyper-connected age: we have gained an unprecedented breadth of connection, yet we may be losing the depth of it; we have more "social interaction," yet experience far less "genuine engagement."

The most ingenious design of digital socializing—and also its greatest trap—lies in how it simplifies complex, ambiguous, and ineffable human emotions into clear, quantifiable metrics. "Likes," "follower counts," "shares," "friend counts"—these numbers have become intuitive benchmarks for us to measure our social value and popularity. We find ourselves chasing the rise and fall of these numbers like stock prices; a red notification badge can trigger a surge of dopamine.

But can this quantified social currency really be exchanged for genuine emotional fulfillment? Psychologist Sherry Turkle cuts to the core of the issue: we are shifting from a culture of "conversation" to a culture of "connection." Conversation is slow, spontaneous, and filled with unpredictability. It demands our full attention, and requires us to embrace silence, awkwardness, and disagreement. Connection, by contrast, is efficient, concise, and controllable. We prefer sending a WeChat message over making a phone call; we'd rather hit "like" than write a thoughtful comment. The former costs less and carries less risk.

Thus, we find ourselves in a predicament: we have hundreds of people we can "connect" with, yet barely a few with whom we can have a deep "conversation." We use busyness in breadth to mask our lack in depth. As a friend who stays active in over a dozen WeChat groups put it: "It feels like I'm talking to everyone, yet at the same time, talking to no one. The excitement belongs to them— I have nothing." This model of replacing qualitative engagement with quantitative interaction creates an illusion of intimacy. It satisfies our hunger for social contact, yet never truly nourishes the soul that craves to be deeply understood and seen.

Human emotional bonds have always been "embodied" since ancient times. A comforting hug, a knowing glance, a high-five between friends, a gentle touch of lovers' fingertips—these non-verbal, physical exchanges carry even richer emotional messages than words themselves. They activate our mirror neurons, bringing a sense of security, belonging, and empathy.

Digital connection, by its very nature, is a "disembodied" experience. No matter how advanced the technology, an emoji cannot replace a real smile; a "hug" sticker cannot convey body warmth or a heartbeat. We see the other person's image in a video call, yet cannot share the scent and atmosphere of the same physical space. This "sensory deprivation" style of communication is like eating freeze-dried food: it provides basic nutrition, but loses the color, aroma, taste, and chewing satisfaction of fresh ingredients.

Most worrying of all, this social habit of "physical absence" is conversely eroding our ability to engage with others in real life. In a café, a couple sits across from each other, yet both bury their heads in their phones; at a family gathering, with children and grandchildren all around, people are more eager to post photos to Moments for likes than to talk to the relatives beside them. Our bodies are present, but our emotions and attention have wandered "to the cloud." We are lonely together. The "Device Paradigm" proposed by technology philosopher Albert Borgmann becomes evident here: technological devices (such as mobile phones) provide us with convenient services (connection), yet at the same time hide and strip away the associated social practices, skills, and experiences—such as deep conversation and the ability to be present with others. We gain the outcome of connection, but lose the rich meaning brought by the process of connecting.

The flip side of hyper-connectivity is emotional energy overload. In the pre-digital era, returning home from work meant a temporary pause on work-related social interactions. Today, however, WeChat work groups, Moments, and email notifications are always online. Our social lives have shifted from "dramas" with clear beginnings and endings to a never-ending "soap opera." This demand for "constant availability" drains our "emotional bandwidth" nonstop. We are forced to juggle multiple relationships, contexts, and identities simultaneously: one moment playing the role of a filial child in a family group, the next switching to a professional employee in a work group, while also maintaining an engaging persona on Moments. The cognitive load and performance pressure from these frequent context shifts leave people mentally drained. We seem to become 24/7 customer service for our own social networks, on call at all times to meet everyone's expectations.

More subtly, this overload is sometimes a "sweet burden"—we enjoy the feeling of being needed and fear missing out on anything (FOMO), so we actively choose to be "held hostage." Yet this self-exploitative form of connection ultimately leads to profound fatigue and loneliness: we maintain high-intensity but superficial contact with the world, yet mental exhaustion leaves us no time to nurture deep relationships—ones that require time, patience, and vulnerability. We may seem to "own the whole world," but our inner selves can feel empty.

Revealing this paradox is not about rejecting technology, but about using it more consciously. Digital connection itself is not the original sin; the problem arises when we treat it as the sole or central part of our emotional lives, while neglecting other older, simpler forms of connection.

The solution may lie in moving from "unconscious obsession" to "conscious choice"—we need to establish an "ethics of connection" for the digital age. First, we must distinguish between superficial "connection" and deep "engagement." We should understand that likes and comments are merely "social snacks" that provide instant gratification, while long, in-depth conversations and shared in-person experiences are the "emotional main courses" that nourish the soul—and we must deliberately set aside time and energy for the latter. Second, we need to value the irreplaceability of "corporeal presence." We should proactively create opportunities for offline encounters, recognizing that a dinner where phones are put away conveys more warmth through shared body language and eye contact than thousands of fragmented messages. Third, we must courageously refuse "constant availability." Through technological boundaries and mental discipline, we can protect our "sacred time"—moments free from interruptions—to refocus our attention on the present and the people in front of us. Finally, we should shift from passive consumption to active creation. Instead of indulging in browsing others' lives, we can turn social media into a bridge for real encounters: transform online shared interests into offline book clubs, develop "like-based acquaintances" into in-person conversations over coffee, and let technology truly serve our original desire for genuine connection.

The loneliness of hyper-connectivity—this era's emotional paradox—ultimately challenges each of us: in pursuing the efficiency of connection, have we forgotten its original purpose? Connection is meant to enhance encounters, not replace them; to enrich life, not empty it. Perhaps genuine connection does not depend on mastering advanced communication technologies, but on whether we still retain the willingness and ability to put aside all technology, sit quietly with another person, and share their joys and sorrows. Amid endless digital noise, guarding that inner space for deep engagement may be the most precious emotional practice of our time.

Section 3: The Metamorphosis of Self Between Virtual and Real

In the labyrinth woven by digital technology, we are undergoing a profound transformation of the "self." In the "risk society" described by German sociologist Ulrich Beck, individuals are forced to become authors of their own life biographies—and digital technology has elevated this creativity to unprecedented heights. No longer content with our innate, singular identity, we actively engage in a grand experiment of selfhood: heroes in games, experts on social media, outspoken voices in anonymous forums. These avatars allow us to experience multiple lives. Behind this experiment lies the vivid manifestation of French philosopher Gilles Deleuze's "rhizome theory" in the digital age: the self is no longer a tree with a single taproot, but a rhizomatic structure—acentered, nonhierarchical, and in constant connection and reconnection.

Philosophically, this fluidity of identity is not entirely new. Postmodern thinkers have long deconstructed the concept of a fixed, unified self, arguing that identity is always fluid, contextual, and socially constructed. Digital technology, however, has pushed this fluidity to its extreme. In the "liquid modernity" described by sociologist Zygmunt Bauman, identity flows and morphs like a liquid, resisting stable form. Social media platforms serve as the perfect vessels for this liquid identity. We carefully curate different versions of ourselves across platforms: on professional networking sites, we are polished, driven career elites; on photo-sharing apps, we are tasteful connoisseurs of life; on Weibo, we might be incisive commentators on current affairs; in anonymous online communities, we may reveal an entirely different private persona. Each platform acts like a funhouse mirror—selectively amplifying one facet of the self while distorting the whole.

This identity performance is not entirely false; it is more about "selective authenticity." As sociologist Erving Goffman proposed in The Presentation of Self in Everyday Life with his "dramaturgical theory": social interaction resembles a stage play, where we perform on the "front stage" and be ourselves only in the "back stage." Digital socializing, however, uniquely erodes this back stage. Every like, comment, share, and even silence becomes part of our front-stage performance, permanently exposed to potential audiences. We are forced into constant performance, until we can barely distinguish: Which is the performance, and which is our true self? This compels us to ask: When our curated digital avatars gain approval, are we expressing our authentic selves, or catering to others' expectations? When success in the virtual world comes easier than real achievements, will we gradually lose ourselves in digital illusions?

If avatar technology gives us tools to shape the self, algorithms are the invisible directors in this process. Jean-Paul Sartre famously stated "hell is other people," pointing out that we are always defined and objectified under the gaze of others. In the digital age, this "other" has materialized as the algorithmic gaze. Algorithms continuously collect our behavioral data—clicks, dwell time, likes, searches—building data models of "who we are," then reinforcing these models with content we might enjoy. This process mirrors philosopher Louis Althusser's concept of "interpellation": through constant "calling" of certain content, algorithms make us "identify with" and internalize specific identities, ultimately shaping us into who they think we should be.

More profoundly, this identity solidification often occurs unconsciously. We immerse ourselves in algorithmically tailored "filter bubbles," our horizons narrowing by the day. We mistake the world inside the bubble for the full truth, and the personality reinforced within it for our complete self. For instance, a user who initially held moderate views on an issue might gradually turn extreme after being immersed in algorithmically pushed radical content—yet still believe this stance stems from independent thinking. In this way, algorithms not only shape our information environment but also deeply mold our identity, confining the fluid self within a cage of data predictions.

Section 4: Ethical Dilemmas in the Digital Age

"My father passed away two years ago, and his WeChat account has become the most precious digital legacy for our whole family." A netizen named "Time Traveler" shared this on Zhihu, receiving thousands of likes. "Every time I miss him, I open his Moments and listen to the voice messages he sent when he was alive. But recently, I've been having nightmares—dreaming that one day this account will disappear suddenly, as if he's leaving us a second time." This true story reveals an ethical dilemma we will all face sooner or later: when digital immortality becomes technologically feasible, how should we accommodate humanity's fragility and emotions? We are experiencing a "temporal-spatial dislocation" in ethics: technology advances at the speed of light, while ethical understanding lags behind at a walking pace. When children of the younger generation skillfully give commands to smart speakers, we can't help but wonder: they may think the world has always been this way—every action recorded, every preference predicted, every relationship digitized. But does this natural adaptation of "digital natives" also mean they will unknowingly surrender more fundamental rights?

The convenience of digital connection often comes at the cost of relationship depth. When making friends only requires a "right swipe," saying goodbye just a "block," and showing sympathy merely a "like," human relationships seem reduced to lightweight, quickly consumable products. This "lightweighting" eliminates the burdens of relationships, but also drains their weight. Ethicists worry this trend is eroding the foundation of social morality—responsibility. Philosopher Emmanuel Levinas argued that ethics arises from the infinite responsibility evoked when facing the "Other." That specific, irreducible "face" demands my response and my responsibility. Yet in digital interactions, the "Other" is easily simplified to an avatar, a paragraph of text, or an opinion. We find it easier to ignore the "Other" and avoid the weight of responsibility. Cyberbullying is the most extreme example: perpetrators do not face a person who bleeds or suffers, but merely a dissatisfying symbol.

German philosopher Heinrich Schweitzer once asked: In the post-secular age, where will humanity's spirituality go? This question becomes exceptionally concrete in the digital age. A netizen wrote on Weibo: "My grandfather was a carpenter. After he died, we could still

135

run our hands over the furniture he crafted with his own hands and feel the warmth he left in the world. But when our generation passes away, what we leave behind may only be a cold cloud of data—can they really carry our souls?"

This question hits the core of the digital legacy dilemma. In 2018, the German Federal Supreme Court ruled to allow parents to inherit their deceased daughter's Facebook account, setting a precedent for digital legacy protection. Yet more ethical questions remain unresolved. A friend of mine, a 32-year-old programmer, wrote a "digital will" last year, explicitly stating: if he dies unexpectedly, he wants his family to immediately delete his browser history and all social media accounts. "Everyone has the right to be imperfect," he said. "I don't want my family to see every side of me online."

This raises a profound ethical question: In the digital age, do we still have the "right to be forgotten"? When technology makes memory eternal, forgetting instead becomes a privilege that must be fought for.

"I trade privacy for convenience—that's the basic transaction rule of this era." A product manager at a tech company made this comment at an industry forum, sparking intense debate. A netizen named "Data Laborer" countered: "The problem is that this transaction has never been fair—we are forced into it without full awareness."

Data privacy issues are even more pervasive. The concept of "surveillance capitalism" proposed by American scholar Shoshana Zuboff accurately depicts the current dilemma: our personal experiences are extracted for free, then converted into behavioral data, and finally used to predict and influence our actions. This process is like an "enclosure movement" of the digital age, privatizing and commercializing personal experiences that originally belonged to the public domain. The European Union's General Data Protection Regulation (GDPR) and China's Personal Information Protection Law attempt to set boundaries for this movement, but the lag of legislation leaves many gray areas unaddressed. When we use free apps, do we truly understand that we are trading privacy for convenience? Is this "consent" actually a forced choice under information asymmetry?

The issue of algorithmic bias has shattered the myth of technological neutrality. During training, machine learning algorithms often inadvertently amplify pre-existing biases in society. American computer scientist Joy Buolamwini discovered that commercial facial recognition systems have a significantly higher error rate when identifying women with darker skin than men with lighter skin—not because the technology itself is biased, but because the training data lacks diversity. As a result, algorithms become amplifiers and rationalizers of structural social inequalities. More worrying is that the "black box" nature of algorithms makes such biases hard to detect and correct. When algorithms decide who qualifies for a loan, who gets parole approval, or whose resume reaches HR, we are essentially ceding critical social decision-making power to an opaque system that may be riddled with biases.

The ethical boundary between human-machine relationships is also growing blurrier. When AI chatbots can provide more immediate emotional support than humans, and lonely elderly people prefer confiding in care robots, we are forced to rethink the essence of relationships. The "anthropocentrism" deconstructed by French philosopher Jacques Derrida now faces practical challenges: If a machine can alleviate human loneliness, is there a fundamental difference between this and comfort provided by humans? Furthermore, do we have the right to abuse or "torture" AI entities— even if they lack the ability to feel pain, could such behavior erode our own moral sensibilities? The answers to these questions will redefine "what it means to be human" and "what it means to be a machine."

Faced with these complex ethical dilemmas, we need to build a multi-layered, dynamically adaptive ethical framework. At the individual level, we must cultivate "digital literacy"—not just the ability to use technology, but also the awareness and capacity to reflect on the ethical impacts behind it. At the societal level, we need a governance model with multi-stakeholder participation, bringing together tech developers, ethicists, policymakers, and public representatives to co-create rules. At the philosophical level, we must return to Immanuel Kant's concept of the "kingdom of ends": never treat ourselves or others merely as means, but always as ends in themselves.

Technological progress is inevitable, but its direction and application depend on our choices. The principle of responsibility ethics proposed by German philosopher Hans Jonas offers a guideline: "Your actions must be compatible with the permanence and authenticity of human life affected by them." In the digital age, this principle means we must remain vigilant about technology's long-term impacts and potential risks—especially those that may be irreversible.

Ultimately, the ethical dilemmas of the digital age boil down to dilemmas of human values. How do we balance efficiency and fairness, convenience and privacy, innovation and stability, global connectivity and cultural diversity? These choices have no one-size-fits-all answers, but they will define the character and warmth of digital civilization. Every time we develop and deploy a new technology, we must keep asking: Does this technology make people more free or more controlled? Does it promote human flourishing or reduce people to data points? Does it foster human solidarity or create new divisions?

The answers lie not in technology itself, but in us—the creators and users of technology. Can we retain moral imagination and ethical courage, never losing sight of human scale amid innovation, and never straying from our value anchors while embracing change? The true "metaverse" should not be a utopia for escaping reality, but a tool for empowering it. It should help people who are lonely due to geographical, physical, or social constraints find belonging—not alienate those who could otherwise embrace each other. It should expand the dimensions of humanity, not diminish the weight of life. Amid the tide of technology, we must remember: the deepest connections always require an open heart, the courage to be vulnerable, and the willingness to invest time. Digital stars may shine brightly, but earthly lights are where we begin and return. Only then can we ensure the digital age is not an era of ethical loss, but one where human values are reborn under the conditions of new technology.

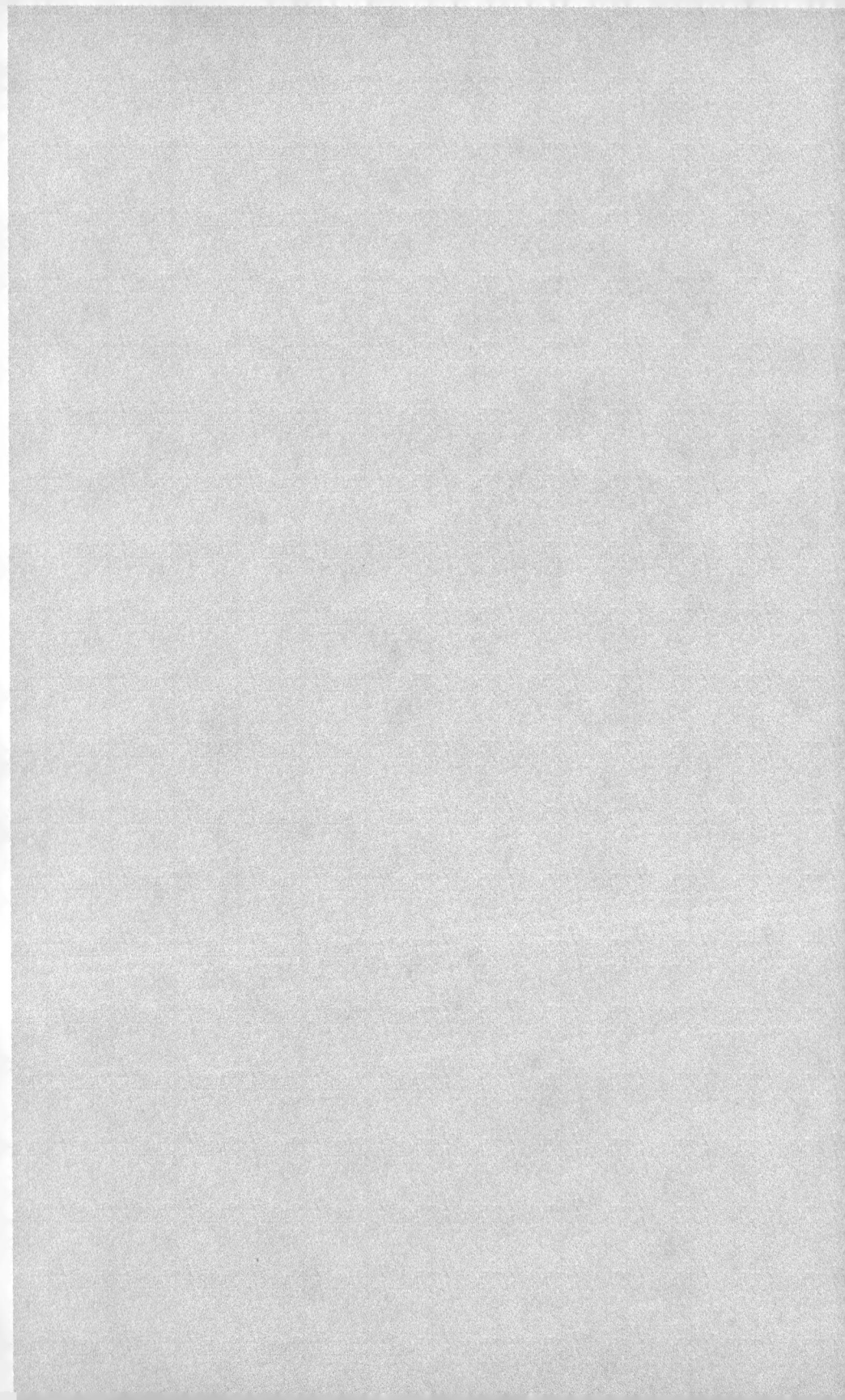

Cognitive Prisoners:
The Self Within Algorithms

1. The Birth of the Information Echo Chamber

2. When Judgment Is Handed to Data Profiles

3. Cognitive Crisis in the Age of Deepfakes

4. The Shackles of Will: Has Freedom Become an Algorithm's Puppet?

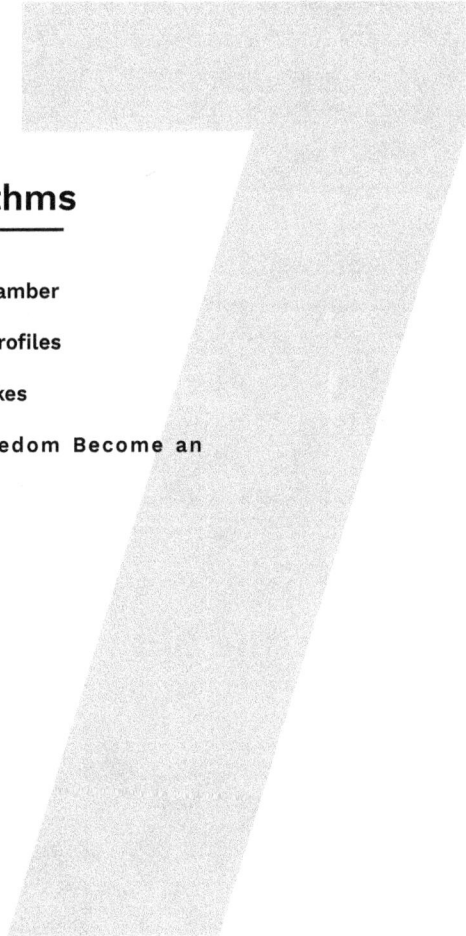

Chapter 7
Cognitive Prisoners: The Self Within Algorithms

We are stepping into a cognitive labyrinth woven by code. Algorithms are no longer cold programs hidden behind screens—they have become an omnipresent "cognitive companion" in our daily lives, quietly shaping how we see the world, how we think, and even defining the ultimate answer to "who I am." This is an era filled with the allure of intelligence yet hiding a crisis of autonomy: we enjoy unprecedented convenience in accessing information, but may pay the price of diminished critical thinking depth; we receive precisely tailored content feeds, but lose the joy of exploring the unknown; we think we are making independent choices, yet we may only be fulfilling propositions pre-set by algorithms. This chapter delves into this data-driven cognitive world, starting from technological mechanisms and moving through psychological, sociological, and philosophical dimensions to pose a question fundamental to humanity: As algorithms grow increasingly intelligent, is our thinking becoming more free, or are we becoming prisoners of our own preferences? Is the subjectivity of cognition being elevated through technological empowerment, or quietly fading away amid intelligent recommendations?

Section 1: The Birth of the Information Echo Chamber

Before the morning sun filters through the curtains, Li Wei has already reached for her phone by the pillow. As the screen lights up, several notifications pop up on time: "A blogger you follow has updated," "Recommendations based on your preferences," "News we think you'll want to see." She skillfully swipes and taps, immersing herself in the algorithm-prepared "information breakfast"—a few articles on career promotion tips, a preview of an art exhibition that matches her taste, and a fitness video from her favorite blogger. Everything fits her preferences perfectly, as if the world was always meant to align with her likes. It is not until a dinner with a long-unseen friend that she realizes something is wrong: the social event her friend discusses enthusiastically is something she has never even heard of. This topic, well-known to everyone in her friend's world, has never appeared in her information feed. In that moment, Li Wei faintly hears the sound of an invisible wall, crashing into place.

We are undergoing an experiment unprecedented in the history of human cognition. In the name of "personalized services," the reach of algorithms has quietly penetrated every link in how we perceive the world. They promise to take us to a broader world, yet unknowingly build a unique cognitive cage for each of us. These walls woven by code are transparent and comfortable, so much so that we often forget they exist—until one day we look up and realize the sky is no longer its original shape.

The emergence of the algorithmic echo chamber is not the "misdoing" of a single technology, but an inevitable result of an entire commercial logic. Silicon Valley was the first to realize that in an era of information explosion, the real scarcity is not information, but human attention. Thus, the "attention economy" became the core engine of internet giants. In this model, users are no longer traditional consumers, but "products" sold to advertisers; our attention duration and click actions are all commodities with clear price tags.

Personalized recommendation algorithms are the most efficient hunting tools under this economic model. Their design purpose is remarkably simple: to maximize user screen time. The optimal strategy to achieve this goal is not to broaden users' horizons, but to precisely feed them content they like the most. Ed Felten, a computer scientist at Yale University, once pointed out sharply: "These systems are not designed to help you learn new things; they are designed to keep you engaged." Just like a casino slot machine that keeps people inserting coins through intermittent small rewards, algorithms keep us lingering in repeated "pleasure of recognition" by continuously providing content that aligns with our preferences.

This mechanism finds a counterpart in neuroscience. When we see content that matches our views, the brain's reward circuit is activated, releasing dopamine and creating a sense of pleasure. Conversely, information that challenges our existing cognition triggers a response in the anterior insula, bringing discomfort similar to physical pain. Algorithms have unknowingly become precise controllers of our dopamine circuits—they constantly reinforce our existing preferences and avoid any content that might cause cognitive discomfort. We think we are making free choices, but in reality, we have already become prisoners of our own neural mechanisms, and algorithms are the wardens who know our weaknesses best.

The filtering mechanism of algorithms creates a paradox: the seemingly boundless universe of information is actually shrinking dramatically. In 2011, internet activist Eli Pariser first voiced this concern in his book The Filter Bubble. He revealed the severity of the problem through a simple experiment: he asked two friends with different political leanings to search for "BP" simultaneously. One received investment information about British Petroleum, while the other got news about the Deepwater Horizon oil spill environmental disaster. Based on its judgment of user profiles, the algorithm had already decided in advance what "the facts you should know" were.

The terrifying aspect of this information filtering lies in its invisibility. Traditional news editors have their own agenda-setting processes, but at least their criteria are publicly discernible. The decision-making process of algorithms, however, remains hidden in an opaque black box. We neither know which information has been filtered out nor understand the criteria behind the filtering. More worrying is that this filtering is extending from the online world to the offline realm. While navigation apps plan the "fastest route" for us, they also filter out the alleys where we might stumble upon unexpected scenery; food delivery platforms recommend restaurants "you might like," making us stop exploring that unassuming yet delightful family diner around the corner; music streaming services constantly reinforce our listening preferences, causing us to miss music genres that could open doors to new worlds. The world shrinks before us into an increasingly narrow pipeline, yet we mistakenly believe this represents the full breadth of the world.

The progress of human cognition relies heavily on accidental encounters with the unknown. Many major breakthroughs in the history of science stemmed from unexpected discoveries—Alexander Fleming's penicillin, Wilhelm Conrad Röntgen's X-rays, Arno Penzias and Robert Wilson's cosmic microwave background radiation— all were unplanned gifts. Sociologist Robert Merton termed this phenomenon "serendipity"—the fortunate occurrence of unexpected discoveries.

The algorithm-dominated information environment is systematically stifling these "unexpected encounters." Taylor Owen, director of the Center for Digital Media Research at Columbia University, warns: "When we hand over all decisions to algorithms that prioritize maximum efficiency, we are essentially sacrificing society's ability to learn." Social learning requires exposure to diverse perspectives, experience of cognitive conflict, and groping through uncertainty. The cognitive comfort zone provided by algorithms deprives us of such learning opportunities.

This harm is particularly evident in education. Adaptive learning systems can provide customized exercises based on each student's ability level. While this seems to improve efficiency, it also deprives students of the chance to tackle difficult problems and experience setbacks. Educators at the University of California, Irvine, found that students overly dependent on personalized learning systems demonstrate significantly lower problem-solving abilities and resilience when faced with novel problems not covered by the system. Algorithms clear all the "gravel" from our cognitive path, yet in doing so, they rob us of the ability to learn how to overcome obstacles.

In the 1960s, philosopher Herbert Marcuse depicted in One-Dimensional Man how advanced industrial societies, through the provision of abundant goods and entertainment, make people content with the status quo and lose the ability to think critically and dissent. He would hardly have imagined that half a century later, algorithms would take this "one-dimensional" shaping to an extreme. The most profound harm of the algorithmic echo chamber is not that it prevents us from seeing opposing views, but that it makes us no longer need opposing views. In the era of traditional media, even if you read a newspaper with a clear partisan stance, you would at least be aware of the existence of other positions. In the algorithm-created information environment, however, dissenters are not only filtered out—their very existence is concealed. We immerse ourselves in content that constantly reinforces our existing views, gradually forming a cognitive closed loop: the world is exactly as I see it, because what I see is the entire world.

This closed loop ultimately leads to the atrophy of critical thinking. When all the information we encounter continuously confirms our existing cognition, we no longer need to question, analyze, or argue.

Political scholars have found that people living in highly homogeneous information environments not only struggle to understand the logic of opposing views but even lose the ability to accurately describe the other side's positions. What they construct is often a "cartoon version" of opposing views—a straw man that is easy to refute. The reason many debates on social media end up as talking past each other lies in the fact that the two sides of the debate actually live in parallel realities constructed by different algorithms.

Faced with the siege of the algorithmic echo chamber, completely rejecting technology is not only futile but also a form of anti-intellectual romanticism. The real solution does not lie in destroying algorithms, but in cultivating a form of cognitive literacy for the digital age—an ability to coexist with algorithms without being enslaved by them.

First and foremost, cognitive awakening is needed—recognizing the existence of the "walls." Just as Li Wei suddenly discovered the cognitive gap during her conversation with a friend, we need to proactively seek such "breakthrough moments." We can intentionally follow several high-quality information sources with vastly different perspectives, use privacy-respecting search engines for occasional "aimless browsing," or regularly engage in in-depth conversations with friends from diverse backgrounds. These actions are like opening a window in the algorithm's walls, allowing us to glimpse the world outside.

Technology itself can also be part of the solution. Some developers are creating "anti-recommendation" tools—such as browser plugins that deliberately display random content to break filter bubbles; the "algorithmic transparency" provisions in the EU's Digital Services Act force platforms to explain the basic principles behind content recommendations. These attempts, though elementary, point the way forward: we can demand that algorithms serve us, rather than dominate our cognition. Most importantly, we need to reshape our cognitive habits. Philosopher Daniel Dennett proposed a four-step approach to critical thinking: first, express the other person's viewpoint in its strongest possible form; second, list the points you agree with; third, explain what you have learned from the other person; finally, offer criticism only after completing these three steps.

This way of thinking is particularly valuable in the algorithmic age—it forces us out of our cognitive comfort zones and encourages us to engage sincerely with different perspectives. The algorithm's walls will not disappear, but we can learn to recognize them, cross them, and ultimately move freely both inside and outside. Cognitive autonomy has never been granted by others; it must be earned through continuous conscious practice. In the age of algorithms, being a conscious, autonomous thinker may be the most important intellectual challenge and moral responsibility of our time. When we can enjoy the convenience of algorithms without losing the courage to explore the unknown, we will truly achieve co-evolution with technology—not slowly suffocating inside the algorithm's echo chamber.

Section 2: When Judgment Is Handed to Data Profiles

Inside a conference room at an internet company in Hangzhou, a product manager was demonstrating the latest user profiling system. "Based on our algorithm," he said confidently as he flipped through the PPT slides, "this user has an 87.3% probability of being an urban elite female who prefers light luxury brands, focuses on parenting knowledge, and may be preparing to buy a house soon." A detailed user profile appeared on the screen—covering everything from consumption preferences and life stage to political leanings and emotional traits. Yet all this was derived solely from the user's search history and shopping behavior over the past week. Everyone present marveled at the algorithm's precision, but no one asked the most critical question: Is this "her" defined by data the real her?

We are undergoing an unprecedented revolution in self-perception. Through the fragments we leave in the digital world, algorithms piece together a "data self"—and this virtual image is now reshaping the real us. This quiet process is profoundly altering humanity's most fundamental mode of existence: our relationship with ourselves.

Descartes' "Cogito, ergo sum" ("I think, therefore I am") laid the foundation for modern philosophical subjectivity, asserting that human self-awareness exists through thinking. Today, however, we seem to be slipping toward a new paradigm: "The algorithm knows, therefore I am." Algorithms "know" who we are through data analysis, thereby defining our existence. Behind this shift lies a crisis of the concept of "subjectivity" in Western philosophy. Michel Foucault predicted the "death of man" in The Order of Things, arguing that "man" is merely a knowledge construct of a specific historical era. Algorithms are now accelerating this process—deconstructing living humans into quantifiable, predictable data points. When we begin to understand ourselves through algorithmic feedback, are we experiencing a form of subjective alienation?

This alienation feels particularly contradictory within the context of Chinese culture. Traditional Chinese thought emphasizes "self-reflection" and "self-cultivation," viewing self-perception as an inward exploratory process. But algorithms have externalized this process—we now rely on external data feedback to understand ourselves. As one interviewee put it: "Sometimes I have to look at the recommendation page to figure out what I 'should' like lately."

The "looking-glass self" theory proposed by sociologist Charles Cooley argues that people's self-concepts form through interactions with others; we know ourselves through the mirror of other people. Today, algorithms have become the most important mirror—and it is an intelligently distorted one. This digital mirror has three key traits: first, it is one-way—algorithms observe us, but we cannot see into algorithms; second, it is selective—it only reflects certain aspects of our behavior; third, it is utilitarian—the content it reflects serves commercial purposes. In front of such a mirror, what we see is inevitably a distorted version of ourselves.

More concerningly, this mirror also keeps "speaking." It does not just show "who you are," but also suggests "who you should be." Prompt phrases like "People who bought this also bought..." and "Users who follow this blogger also follow..." constantly shape our social identity. As one sociologist noted: "Algorithms are becoming new agents of socialization; they are teaching us how to be 'qualified' modern people."

In a culture that values collectivism like China's, the homogenizing effect of algorithms is particularly pronounced. Algorithmic recommendations are based on group behavior data, which essentially reinforces mainstream preferences. Niche or alternative cultural expressions rarely receive recommendations and are gradually marginalized.

Sociologist Erving Goffman's "dramaturgical theory" takes on new dimensions here. He argued that social interaction is like a theater, where everyone performs on the "front stage" and reverts to their true selves in the "back stage." But in the face of algorithms, the line between front and back stages has blurred—every click and every moment of screen time is a performance for algorithms, and algorithms treat all this as the "real" us. Even more alarming is that we have begun performing in the way algorithms expect, because only then can we gain more recommendations, more likes, and more recognition.

Commercial forces skillfully exploit this mechanism. Consumerism colludes with algorithms to constantly create and reinforce desires. You see "People like you are buying this," you are told "This is perfect for you," and you are reminded "Don't miss the limited-time offer."

Under such precise marketing, consumption is no longer about meeting actual needs—it is about confirming the identity defined by algorithms. What you buy matters less than who you become through buying it.

In the face of algorithms' powerful influence, reclaiming the right to define ourselves becomes particularly important. This requires action on three levels: cognitively, we must understand how algorithms work and where "Recommended for you" comes from; behaviorally, we should actively create "algorithmic noise" and occasionally step out of the information echo chamber; fundamentally, we need to maintain the habit of self-reflection and frequently question our true preferences.

In a teahouse in Chengdu, I met an interesting elderly man. He insists on living in the most "old-fashioned" way: reading newspapers instead of news apps, shopping in physical stores instead of online, and taking notes in a notebook instead of phone memos. "I'm not against technology," he explained, "I just don't want to be completely arranged by algorithms. Life should leave room for surprises, for the joy of exploring on my own." His words are thought-provoking. Algorithms do bring convenience, but when convenience comes at the cost of autonomy, we need to re-examine this trade-off. The true self is not formed through passive acceptance, but gradually clarified through active exploration, trial and error, and reflection. This process may be inefficient and full of uncertainty—but it is precisely these "inefficiencies" and "uncertainties" that constitute the unique growth experience of being human.

Amid the tide of algorithms, we need those moments that cannot be quantified: putting down our phones to talk face-to-face with friends; walking into a bookstore and stumbling upon an unexpected good book; traveling to an unfamiliar place to experience a different kind of scenery. These "inefficient" and "imprecise" experiences are exactly our most important resources for resisting algorithmic homogenization. In an era wrapped in data, preserving the integrity of the self may be the most precious form of resistance—and the deepest form of freedom. The true self is not formed through passive acceptance, but gradually clarified through active exploration, trial and error, and reflection. Algorithms do bring convenience, but when convenience comes at the cost of autonomy, we need to re-examine this trade-off. In an era wrapped in data, preserving the integrity of the self may be the most precious form of resistance—and the deepest form of freedom.

Section 3: Cognitive Crisis in the Age of Deepfakes

The foundation of humanity's cognitive system is undergoing an unprecedented earthquake. For centuries, we have understood the world through sensory evidence—and visual information in particular has always held "privilege" in judging truth. "Seeing is believing" is not merely a proverb, but a fundamental assumption of human epistemology. Yet the emergence of deepfake technology is shaking this cognitive cornerstone that has endured for millennia. When any image or audio can be flawlessly forged by artificial intelligence, we suddenly find ourselves trapped in a cognitive fog—all the familiar signposts of truth begin to blur. At the core of this cognitive crisis lies a shift in "the right to define authenticity." Traditionally, authenticity was determined by both the inherent properties of facts and social consensus; but in the age of deepfakes, judging authenticity increasingly relies on technical means. We must use one set of algorithms to detect the forged outputs of another. This infinite cycle of verification makes the cognitive process unprecedentedly complex and fragile—when the verification tools themselves require verification, the foundation of cognition begins to shake.

The Fading of Authenticity: From Verification to Doubt

The most profound impact of deepfake technology is fostering a pervasive skepticism toward all digital content. This resembles what psychologists call "truth decay"—not skepticism about a specific fact, but a shaking of the entire cognitive framework .

This phenomenon is particularly evident among young people. A 2023 study by Peking University found that Generation Z has significantly lower trust in digital content than previous generations. "We grew up in the era of Photoshop and filters," one college student admitted. "We've long been accustomed to the possibility that everything could be fake." This widespread doubt may seem like a protective mechanism, but it can lead to more dangerous outcomes: when people cannot distinguish truth from falsehood, they may choose to believe content that best aligns with their expectations—or simply reject believing anything at all.

Jean Baudrillard's "simulacra theory" appears prophetic here.

His concept of "hyperreality"—where simulations become more real than reality itself—is becoming a technological reality. When forged content is more perfect and meets expectations better than the real thing, people are more willing to believe the simulation. This is not because people are foolish, but because human cognition is inherently drawn to consistency and rationality—and algorithm-generated content is often more "reasonable" than messy reality.

The Reconstruction of Trust Systems

Deepfake technology is forcing a reconstruction of society's entire trust system. Traditional trust was built on verifiable chains of evidence, but when evidence itself can be forged, trust must find new foundations.

In the legal realm, evidence rules are evolving. In 2022, the Supreme People's Court issued the Provisions on Several Issues Concerning Online Litigation, which for the first time clarified standards for examining electronic evidence and required special scrutiny of audio-visual materials that may be forged . A judge from a local court told me: "We now focus more on mutual corroboration between pieces of evidence, rather than the probative value of a single piece of evidence."

The news industry is also exploring new trust mechanisms. Xinhua News Agency has experimented with using blockchain technology to add digital watermarks to news images, allowing readers to verify the authenticity and source of images by scanning a QR code. Yet this technical solution faces a fundamental dilemma: when the verification tools themselves require verification, we fall into an infinite cycle of doubt.

The Politics of Memory

The most disturbing applications of deepfakes are concentrated in the tampering of memory narratives and the struggle for power—whether it involves the collective memory of an entire society or the private memory of an individual, the foundation of their authenticity has become fragile under technological impact. The distortion of memory is essentially a reshaping of the right to narrate the past, which in turn affects current social consensus and individual rights.

From the perspective of collective memory, digital carriers of historical narratives face the risk of tampering. Key historical events that shape national identity and social values—such as major revolutionary processes, anti-aggression struggles, and civil rights movements—have preserved video clips, audio recordings, and digital documents. Once modified by deepfake technology, these materials may erode the authentic core of collective memory. For example, altering details of historical figures' words and deeds, adjusting the timeline of historical events, or even fabricating non-existent "historical scenes" can skew the public's understanding of history. This makes society more vulnerable to exploitation by historical revisionism, undermining consensus on the past and shaking the cohesion formed through shared historical memory. More critically, as original digital archives are gradually lost due to storage technology iterations, and tampered "fake memory versions" become mainstream through dissemination advantages, collective memory will fall into the predicament of "distorted inheritance," where future generations' understanding of history may deviate from the essence of facts.

Personal memory is equally at risk, often directly tied to real-world rights. In legal disputes, digital evidence carrying personal experiences—such as home videos, meeting recordings, and call logs—may be tampered with using deepfake technology and presented as courtroom evidence, interfering with judicial judgments. In social contexts, if images of personal growth records or important life milestones (such as graduations or weddings) are maliciously altered and spread, they not only distort an individual's perception of their own experiences but may also trigger identity confusion. More alarmingly, psychological research has long confirmed the inherent plasticity of human memory—when we recall the past, we unconsciously integrate external information to revise our memories. When external digital "evidence" is also contaminated, individuals will struggle to distinguish between real experiences and forged content, falling into "memory disorientation": unable to trust their own memories or rely on external evidence, they may ultimately develop fundamental doubts about the authenticity of their own past.

Reconstruction of Cognitive Ethics

Facing the challenges of deepfakes, we need to establish a new cognitive ethics. This ethics is not only about norms for technology use, but more about how we understand the world and build trust with others.

First, we must acknowledge the limitations of human cognition. We need to learn to coexist with uncertainty—while maintaining necessary skepticism, we must also avoid falling into total skepticism. This requires cultivating a new form of cognitive resilience: the ability to endure cognitive discomfort and make judgments even when evidence is incomplete.

Second, we should rebuild process-based trust. When we cannot fully trust a specific piece of content, we can instead trust the process that produced it—trusting media with strict review mechanisms, and research institutions that prioritize transparency. This trust is not blind; it is based on recognition of their workflows and oversight systems.

Finally, we must preserve the critical perspective of humanism. Technical detection can identify forged traces, but only human holistic judgment can perceive the "sense of authenticity" in content. A senior documentary director told me: "True authenticity does not lie in perfect pixels, but in those unquantifiable details: the subtle changes in gaze, the incoherence in tone, the traces of humanity that algorithms still cannot fully simulate."

Section 4: The Shackles of Will: Has Freedom Become an Algorithm's Puppet?

After algorithms weave information echo chambers, shape data-driven selves, and blur the boundaries of truth, their influence ultimately tightens like a fine net around the core of human cognition—free will. We once saw algorithms as "thoughtful life assistants": pushing news that matches our tastes in the morning, recommending preferred restaurants for lunch, planning optimal routes during commutes, and even preparing "recommended for you" short videos before bed. This "seamless" convenience made us gradually accustomed to life wrapped in algorithms, yet unknowingly, we quietly surrendered our right to "independent choice."

This "passive freedom" essentially represents algorithms pushing the age-old concept of "determinism" into a new era of precision. In the history of philosophy, debates have long raged over the boundary between free will and determinism: genes, environment, and education influence choices, but these influences are often vague and indirect. The emergence of algorithms has shattered this "indirectness"—they no longer merely "influence choices," but "design the soil in which choices grow." This resembles psychologist B.F. Skinner's "operant conditioning chamber": a rat receives food when it presses a lever, and over time, it actively repeats this action; algorithms similarly train our behavior through a comparable "stimulus-response" cycle: clicking on certain videos brings immediate entertainment pleasure, buying recommended products saves selection time, and following navigation routes avoids the anxiety of getting lost. Each positive feedback subtly reinforces the behavioral pattern of "obeying the algorithm," until we form a conditioned reflex—not that we "cannot" deviate from the algorithm, but that we "unwillingly" bear the risk of "wrong choices" and the cost of "independent decision-making."

More alarmingly, behind this "training" lies the core logic of surveillance capitalism (a term coined by Shoshana Zuboff)—the algorithmic manipulation of will essentially transforms "human decision-making" into predictable, monetizable data assets. Every "willing" click, dwell time, and purchase we make provides training data for the algorithm's predictive models; these models then optimize manipulation strategies in return, forming a closed loop of "data collection → behavior prediction → will guidance → further data collection." For instance, internal data from an e-commerce platform in Hangzhou showed that by adjusting product display order (placing high-profit items in the top three positions on the homepage), modifying promotional copy (changing "price reduction" to "exclusive benefit"), and even fine-tuning the color of the payment button (red yields 23% higher click rates than blue), user purchase conversion rates could increase by nearly 40%. When we rejoice at "grabbing an exclusive discount," we may never realize: this "cost-effective choice" was an algorithmically designed commercial strategy from the very start.

Algorithmic manipulation of will also presents a progressive chain from "crude to refined," with each step quietly compressing the space for independent choice. At the most basic level, "recommendations" merely define the scope of options for us—the "Daily Recommendation" on music apps seems to expand music choices, yet in reality filters out genres the algorithm deems "you won't like"; next comes "nudging," which guides decisions through interface design details: food delivery platforms pre-check "order topping for full reduction," making us unknowingly buy unnecessary items; travel apps set a certain ride type as the "default recommendation," which most users confirm directly; video apps enable "autoplay next episode," keeping us up late in the inertia of "just one more episode"— these designs are not "coercive," but exploit human laziness and inertia, making us accept algorithmic arrangements unconsciously.

Going a step deeper is "fine-tuning," where algorithms use massive data to accurately identify human psychological weaknesses and maximize manipulation effects in the name of "science." A social platform once conducted an experiment: changing the "Follow" button to "Join Us" increased new user follow rates by 19%; changing "Share" to "Share with Friends" boosted reposts by 25%. Behind these seemingly minor adjustments lies precise grasp of human social psychology—"Join Us" awakens a sense of belonging, while "Share with Friends" lowers social barriers. The most thorough form of manipulation, however, is "predictive control": before we even become aware of our own needs, algorithms have already prepared solutions. When navigation routes are congested, our first reaction is to "wait for the algorithm to re-plan" rather than independently thinking of alternative paths; when hesitant about shopping, we subconsciously open "Recommended for You" and treat algorithmic suggestions as the "optimal solution"; even when choosing hobbies, we refer to "what users like you are following," equating group preferences with our own choices.

Within this manipulation chain, the "collectivism" and "herd mentality" in Chinese cultural context make algorithmic shackles even more hidden. We are accustomed to "following the choices of the majority," and algorithms exploit this perfectly—by displaying "90% of users chose this" or "people like you are buying this," they make us feel "following the algorithm won't go wrong." For example, during the Spring Festival homeward-bound navigation, even though shorter back roads exist, the algorithm's recommendation of "the route most people choose" leads to widespread highway congestion; even though more distinctive local dishes are available, food delivery platforms' recommendation of "restaurants with the highest sales" gradually pushes niche eateries into obsolescence. This "algorithm-led conformity" not only compresses individual choice space, but also erodes social diversity—when everyone chooses similar products, similar content, and similar lifestyles based on algorithmic recommendations, we fall into a "gentle homogenization," yet still mistake this for the result of "free choice."

The ultimate dilemma in this battle for will lies not in algorithms "making choices for us," but in our equating "being guided by algorithms" with "free choice," even regarding algorithmic arrangements as the "optimal solution." We enjoy the meticulous care of the algorithm "nanny": no need to bother planning travel routes, no need to hesitate over dinner options, no need to sift through massive information for key points—the algorithm organizes everything neatly. But the cost of this convenience is the gradual fading of our impulse to explore the world independently. In the 1960s, Herbert Marcuse wrote in One-Dimensional Man that advanced industrial society uses commodities and entertainment to make people content with the status quo and lose critical thinking; half a century later, algorithms have pushed this "one-dimensionality" to its extreme—they do not use violence to strip us of freedom, but use comfortable confinement to make us voluntarily give it up; they do not deprive us of the right to choose, but make us lose the courage to "choose not to be guided by algorithms."

Technology itself is neither good nor evil, and the "shackles" of algorithms are not unbreakable. The key lies in our willingness to balance convenience and freedom—enjoying algorithmic efficiency without losing the courage to explore independently; relying on algorithmic assistance without surrendering control over our own will. As philosopher Hannah Arendt put it: "Freedom is not a state, but an action." In the age of algorithms, free will is not about "rejecting algorithms," but about "not being defined by them"—when we can maintain critical thinking amid algorithmic recommendations, actively choose beyond default options, and attempt to break through predicted outcomes, we will not become algorithms' puppets, but "autonomous beings" coexisting with algorithms. After all, algorithms can predict our behaviors, but cannot replace us in experiencing the weight of choice; they can plan routes for us, but cannot deprive us of the right to take detours. And this "weight of choice" and "right to take detours" are the final line of defense for human subjectivity, and our most powerful weapon against the fate of being "cognitive prisoners."

A Midfield Retrospect on Human-Machine Symbiosis

If we pause for a moment amid the cognitive fog woven by algorithms, we will realize the intelligent revolution is no longer a distant technological concept—it has permeated every detail of our existence like air. From being gently woken by a smart mattress in the morning, to following the optimal route planned by navigation apps during commutes, to the "recommended for you" content pushed before bed, technology is deeply intertwined with our lives, bodies, and even thoughts in a subtle, unobtrusive way.

We have witnessed tools that once were "passively responsive" gradually gain the ability to perceive the environment and adapt strategies. They can understand our sleep rhythms and adjust our homes to the most comfortable temperature; they can align with our physical needs, using wearable devices to monitor health or even implant technology to compensate for physical defects; they can also integrate into our work and cities—sharing repetitive tasks in the workplace, and making urban pulses clearer through data visualization on city streets. Yet behind this convenience, some confusions have quietly emerged: when smart refrigerators know our dietary preferences and brain-computer interfaces (BCIs) can capture our neural signals, the boundaries of the "self" seem to be blurring; when AI can generate copy and design plans, how should we define our value at work; when virtual social interaction makes connection more convenient, why do we often feel lonely instead; when algorithms filter the information we see and predict our choices, are those seemingly independent decisions actually being quietly guided?

These confusions are never isolated. When technology has shifted from "tools we use" to "the environment that surrounds us," our relationship with it has long transcended the superficial logic of "efficiency improvement" and entered a profound struggle over "what makes us human." We rely on technology to break through physical and cognitive limitations, yet fear losing the ability to make independent judgments in this dependence; we expect technology to bring more equitable opportunities, yet worry it will widen new divides; we enjoy the virtual connections built by technology, yet crave to hold onto the warmth in real relationships. Just as we take the initiative to turn off certain recommendations to break the information echo chamber, or refuse unnecessary permissions to protect privacy—these small choices are essentially about finding a balance between "technological empowerment" and "protection of humanity."

Ultimately, these contradictions hidden in daily life all point to a single core: in the age of intelligence, how should we maintain control over ourselves, ensuring technology always serves human needs rather than defining our lives in reverse? This question is the starting point of the "intelligence paradox" we will explore in depth next—it concerns the distribution of power, the boundaries of equity, and more importantly, the future direction of human civilization.

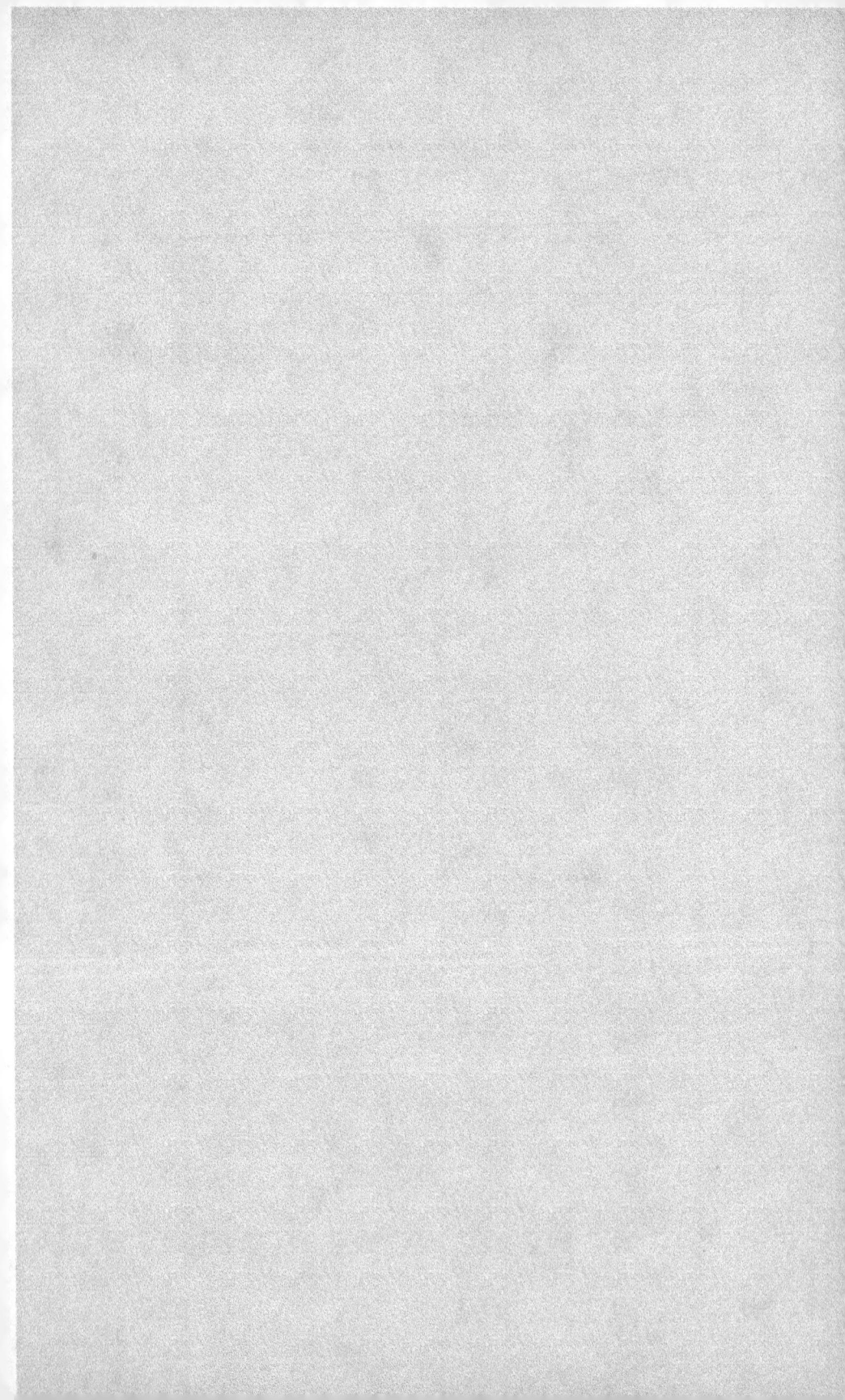

The Intelligence Paradox: Power, Equity, and the Future – Deconstructing Contradictions and Making Civilizational Choices in the Age of AI

1. Re-examining the Transformation: The Multidimensional Penetration of the Intelligent Revolution and the Convergence of Core Contradictions

2. Delving into the Paradoxes: Four Foundational Paradoxes of the Intelligent Age

3. Deconstructing the Challenges: Four Core Hurdles in Reconstructing the Intelligent Order

4. Future Prospects: A Multi-layered Action Framework for Human-Led Transformation

5. The Civilizational Choice: Towards a New Civilizational Form of "Human-Machine Symbiosis"

Chapter 8
The Intelligence Paradox: Power, Equity, and the Future – Deconstructing Contradictions and Making Civilizational Choices in the Age of AI

The wave of intelligent technology has swept into every corner of life. While generously promising efficiency, convenience, and connection, it has also thrust a series of profound paradoxes before us. We enjoy highly personalized services at the cost of the silent erosion of privacy; society achieves leaps in overall efficiency, yet risks exacerbating class and regional inequalities; we are more connected than ever, yet our inner selves experience deeper loneliness and cognitive constraints. This chapter serves as the book's speculative peak, systematically gathering these pervasive contradictions and distilling them into ultimate choices concerning power, equity, and the direction of civilization: In this intelligent revolution, initiated by humanity yet seemingly reshaping humanity in turn, are we the masters, or are we gradually becoming appendages of our own creation? Is the next step for civilization towards technological authoritarianism, or human-machine symbiosis?

Section 1: Re-examining the Transformation: The Multidimensional Penetration of the Intelligent Revolution and the Convergence of Core Contradictions

We are currently in the midst of an unprecedented tide of the intelligent revolution. From the approaching technological singularity depicted in Chapter 1 "The Awakening of Intelligence" to the concrete future visions presented in subsequent chapters, artificial intelligence is no longer a distant concept confined to laboratories. Instead, much like electricity and the Internet, it has become a foundational force that permeates and reshapes every capillary of human society. It promises an unprecedentedly efficient, convenient, and personalized "brave new world." Yet, as each previous chapter has gradually revealed, every leap forward in technology, while solving old problems, inevitably gives rise to new and more complex contradictions. This chapter systematically "reviews" these scattered topics, focusing the brilliant spectrum of technology on the core shadows it casts on the foundation of civilization: How is power distributed? Is society equitable? What is the value of humanity? These contradictions await our analysis.

As the opening section of this chapter, its core task is to examine the extensive transformations discussed in the first seven chapters within the dynamic interaction framework of "technology-human-environment," and from this, extract three major "contradiction clusters": the imbalance between convenience and privacy in the dimension of daily life, the disconnect between efficiency and fairness in the social dimension, and the conflict between connection and autonomy in the dimension of human cognition. These three clusters do not emerge out of thin air; they are inevitable products of the multi-dimensional penetration of the intelligent revolution, laying a solid factual foundation for our subsequent deconstruction of the deeper "intelligence paradox."

Life Dimension: The Imbalance Between Convenience and Privacy – "Who is in charge of my life?"

The most intuitive penetration of the intelligent revolution occurs in our daily living spaces. Chapters 2 ("Future Dwellings") and 3 ("The Body Revolution") jointly sketch a vision of a "Proactive Environment": our homes and bodies are no longer passive objects but intelligent terminals capable of sensing, predicting, and proactively meeting our needs.

For instance, Xiaomi's smart mattress can continuously monitor a user's sleep quality, heart rate, respiratory rate, and even sense tossing and turning, automatically adjusting room temperature, lighting, and humidity to create an optimal sleep environment. Samsung's Smart Family Hub refrigerator not only manages ingredient inventory and suggests recipes but can also identify food items via a built-in camera and automatically place restocking orders on e-commerce platforms. On the bodily level, Iceland's Össur Proprio smart bionic prosthesis, equipped with sensors and AI algorithms, can analyze the user's walking intent and terrain changes in real-time, providing near-natural tactile feedback and adaptive adjustments, significantly enhancing the user's quality of life.

These technological examples vividly embody the pinnacle of "convenience": the environment acts like an omniscient butler, fulfilling needs before we even voice them. However, the price for this convenience is the comprehensive datafication and externalization of the personal "sphere of self." Our sleep habits, physiological rhythms, dietary preferences, and even the subtlest movement patterns of our bodies are transformed into continuous data streams, uploaded to the cloud, and parsed and stored by algorithms. This triggers a fundamental conflict: when the "intelligent environment" perpetually monitors for the sake of prediction, where are the boundaries of humanity's last private domains? The bedroom and the body, traditionally the most intimate realms belonging to the "self," have now become the front lines of data collection. We gain meticulous convenience but cede our most precious privacy, trapped in a passive transaction of "trading data for comfort." This "Convenience-Privacy" contradiction is the primary ripple stirred as intelligent technology penetrates to the core of personal life.

Societal Dimension: The Rift Between Efficiency and Equity – "Who shares the dividends of growth?"

The penetration of the intelligent revolution extends far beyond individual life, profoundly impacting the macro-structure of society and the economy. Chapters 4 ("The New Species in the Workplace") and 5 ("The City Brain") concentrated demonstrate AI's immense power in enhancing the overall operational efficiency of society.

In the workplace, AI creative assistance tools (such as ChatGPT and Midjourney) are becoming "collaborators" for designers, copywriters, and programmers, significantly improving the efficiency of creative production. Meanwhile, industrial robots and automated assembly lines have almost completely replaced repetitive, process-oriented manual labor, pushing production efficiency to the extreme. At the urban level, intelligent governance systems represented by Hangzhou's "Urban Brain" can dynamically adjust the duration of

166

traffic lights by conducting real-time analysis of the city's traffic flow data, successfully increasing the peak-hour traffic efficiency in key areas by over 20%. Additionally, intelligent job-matching platforms aim to achieve accurate and efficient matching between the labor force and job demands.

These achievements exemplify the logic of "efficiency first": intelligent systems can optimize resource allocation at speeds and precision far surpassing human capabilities. However, technology's "optimal solution" is not synonymous with society's "equitable solution." The distribution of efficiency gains exhibits a pronounced "Matthew Effect." Technology monopolies, leveraging barriers of data and algorithms, amass enormous profits, intensifying the concentration of wealth in a few tech hubs. Simultaneously, the widespread adoption of industrial robots may lead to a sharp decline in employment opportunities in traditional manufacturing regions, while intelligent job-matching systems, often due to insufficient digital infrastructure coverage in remote areas and biases in data samples, can 反而 widen the opportunity gap between regions and different skill groups. The City Brain optimizes traffic on arterial roads, but do the density of its sensor coverage and the priorities of its algorithm optimization unintentionally neglect public service investment in non-core areas and low-income communities?

Thus, we see the emergence of the second contradiction cluster: while society enjoys the massive efficiency gains brought by intelligent technology, the risks of internal structural inequity are simultaneously amplified. The classic proposition of "Efficiency versus Equity" gains new sharpness in the intelligent age: Does technology empower everyone, or merely the already empowered few, Youdaoplaceholder0 leading to the harsh reality of "technological monopolies exacerbating class/regional divides"?

Cognitive Dimension: The Conflict Between Connection and Autonomy – "Do my thoughts still belong to me?"

The most concealed and profound penetration of the intelligent revolution occurs within the human mind. Youdaoplaceholder0 6 ("The Social Metaverse") and 7 ("The Cognitive Prisoner") reveal how AI is reshaping our social patterns and cognitive processes.

Technology promises richer "connections." Virtual idols (such as China's A-SOUL and Japan's Hatsune Miku) have formed unprecedented emotional bonds and community identity with their fans; AR virtual communities allow people to transcend physical limitations, collaborating, entertaining, and socializing in shared digital spaces—as if realizing the ideal of "being neighbors despite being worlds apart."

Yet the foundation of these connections lies in algorithmic frameworks. Chapter 7 sharply points out that the personalized recommendation algorithms (such as the information feeds of TikTok or Toutiao) supporting these experiences, while striving to cater to our preferences, also build increasingly solid "Filter Bubbles" and "echo chambers" around us. Notably, studies have shown that the proportion of users with extreme viewpoints increases significantly among those who rely on algorithms for information long-term. This is because they are continuously pushed content that reinforces their inherent positions, while heterogeneous perspectives are systematically filtered out and blocked.

This triggers the third, and perhaps most critical, contradiction cluster: While intelligent technology constructs unprecedentedly vast virtual connections for us, is it also secretly eroding our capacity for independent thought and autonomous cognition? We seemingly browse, choose, and socialize actively, but in reality, our attention, emotions, and even values are being guided and shaped by invisible algorithms. This "cognitive shackling" makes it difficult to form the common ground necessary for public dialogue, as people increasingly live in meaning worlds constructed by their respective algorithms, worlds that do not interconnect. The illusion of connection and the dissolution of autonomy constitute the core conflict at the level of the human mind in the intelligent age.

We can clearly see that the intelligent revolution is by no means a merely one-dimensional technological advancement. Its penetration across the life, societal, and cognitive dimensions, while bringing enormous benefits, has also systematically converged and intensified three pairs of core contradictions: Convenience vs. Privacy, Efficiency vs. Equity, and Connection vs. Autonomy. These contradictions are not isolated from each other; they collectively point to a more profound, essential question: Is the ultimate goal of intelligent technology to serve human freedom and development, or to alienate humanity into optimizable parameters within data streams, efficiency metrics, and algorithmic models?

Section 2: Delving into the Paradoxes: Four Foundational Paradoxes of the Intelligent Age

The intelligent revolution has not yielded a singular narrative of progress, but rather a complex landscape woven from numerous contradictions. These are not mere accidental technical glitches or easily remedied institutional flaws; they are rooted in the profound tension between the intrinsic logic of intelligent technology and the inherent paradigms of human civilization. This section aims to achieve a cognitive leap from "contradictions" to "paradoxes." Here, a "Paradox" refers to a set of propositions that are simultaneously valid yet mutually opposing, revealing an internal, seemingly irreconcilable logical dilemma within a system. The four fundamental paradoxes of the intelligent age are manifestations of the fundamental conflict that arises when technological evolution reaches a certain stage and clashes with the human subjects it is meant to serve and their social structures. Deconstructing these paradoxes is the speculative cornerstone for understanding our current predicament and seeking a way forward.

The core of the Privacy Paradox lies in the seemingly unbridgeable chasm between our demand for intelligent services and We hold fast To the personal sphere. To obtain highly personalized predictive "proactive environments"—whether it's a smart mattress adjusting room temperature based on sleep data or a smartwatch monitoring physiological metrics in real-time—we must continuously and extensively surrender personal data. Yet, the more thoroughly we surrender data, the more inviolable "sphere of self," which constitutes "being human, atrophies. This is far from a simple transaction of "trading privacy for convenience"; it is a struggle over the "right to self-definition." The more technology attempts to "understand" us to provide better service, the more it must penetrate the privacy barrier, ultimately leading to the continuous dissolution of the subjectivity of the very "self" being served.

The sharpness of this paradox becomes clearer through concrete examples: The Apple Watch continuously tracks user heart rate, blood oxygen, and sleep depth. While this data could be used for early disease warning, its business model might transform these highly sensitive physiological data into a basis for personalized ads or even a reference for insurance companies to assess risk, turning the body's internal state into a resource for commercial exploitation. Technologies like Neuralink's brain-computer interfaces push this to the extreme—they promise to help paralyzed individuals reconnect with the world, yet they also place humanity's last sanctuary of privacy—the electrochemical activity of thought and emotion— at risk of being datafied, parsed, and even commercialized. From a philosophical perspective, Heidegger's discourse on technology as "revealing" illuminates the underlying logic: the essence of modern technology is a "challenging-forth" revealing, which forces the world (including humans themselves) to appear as a "standing-reserve" of orderable resources. Intelligent technology is the ultimate manifestation of this logic—it "reveals" the human body, behavior, and even emotions as data streams to be collected, analyzed, and optimized, bringing convenience while simultaneously total infringementing "bodily privacy," a fundamental human existential experience. The traditional concept of a "self" with boundaries and inner secrets gradually dissolves within this panoramic system of monitoring and optimization.

If the Privacy Paradox concerns the human "sphere of self," then the Employment Paradox strikes directly at the foundational value of humans in social production. The core logic of how intelligent technology enhances societal production efficiency is essentially the substitution and optimization of human labor—whether it's GitHub Copilot automating basic programming tasks or IBM Watson for Oncology efficiently analyzing medical images, technology is reconstructing production processes at speeds and precision far surpassing humans. However, for humanity, labor has never been merely a means of livelihood; it is a core space for individuals to integrate into society, create value, gain dignity, and define themselves.Thus, the cruel of the Employment Paradox lies in this: the higher the intelligent efficiency the more the social functions and meaningful value traditionally borne by human labor are squeezed out and hollowed. The future we face may not be one "without work," but one where "work can no longer adequately define human value."

Consider the junior programmer: AI code generation tools may not directly cause their unemployment, but they deprive the path of learning, growth, and proving self-worth through completing foundational tasks, compressing their "value space" into narrow domains. In healthcare, AI-assisted diagnosis systems enhance diagnostic efficiency, but they also rob junior doctors of the process of accumulating experience and building professional confidence by handling common ailments, Youdaoplaceholder0 them either to "race" against the AI or regress into vassals handling the "residual" problems the machines cannot cover. Marx's theory of "alienated labor" finds new relevance here: intelligent technology, as the crystallization of human intellect, through its large-scale application, leads to a deeper alienation of the labor process—labor is alienated from an "end" into a "means." The meaning of work ceases to be creation itself, becoming instead a link in feeding AI systems and optimizing algorithmic efficiency. The value of the laborer is redefined by technology, no longer dependent on skill, experience, or creativity, but on the efficiency of collaboration with AI. This stands in sharp opposition to the sociological logic that "labor is the core mechanism of social integration and individual identity," triggering a widespread crisis of value and identity anxiety.

When technology's impact moves from individual privacy and social employment into the depths of the human mind,the Cognitive Paradox becomes the most concealed yet deadly logical dilemma of the intelligent ag.its root lies in the operational mode of intelligent algorithms:to provide ultimate personalized information convenience,algorithms must continuously learn and cater to individual user preferences;yet, the more personalized and precise the recommendations,the more easily individuals become trapped within "Filter Bubbles" and "Echo Chambers" constructed from past preferences and similar viewpoints.Technology, intended as a bridge connecting humanity, ends up fragmenting us at the cognitive level—while building unprecedentedly vast virtual connections, it simultaneously erodes independent thought and autonomous cognitive capacity.

We need only examine daily information consumption habits: Platforms like Jinri Toutiao or Facebook, whose algorithms aim to "maximize user dwell time," continuously feed conservative users content reinforcing their stance and liberal users viewpoints aligning with their inclinations. Over time, not only does dialogue become difficult, but they seemingly inhabit two entirely different realities, making consensus elusive.The emergence of deepfake technology further completely erodes the foundation of consensus based on "seeing is believing"—when any audio or video can be fabricated, the cornerstone of social trust crumbles. From a cognitive psychology perspective, algorithms do not create the human weakness of "confirmation bias," but they are history's most powerful "amplifier" and "automated executor." They systematically exploit and reinforce the human tendency to accept information conforming to pre-existing beliefs, minimizing the innate human curiosity and possibility of exploring heterogeneous viewpoints. This runs counter to the ideal of a "rational public sphere" advocated since the Enlightenment by thinkers like Habermas—when a civilization lacks a shared cognitive foundation, its capacity for democratic deliberation, collective decision-making, and social solidarity suffers a fatal blow.

If the preceding paradoxes reverberate at the individual and societal levels, the Power Paradox propels us onto a grander stage— the restructuring of the global civilizational landscape. Its core conflict lies in this: On one hand, AI technology follows the law of "scale effects"—larger datasets and massive computing power generally train more powerful models. This naturally drives the concentration of technology, data, and capital into the hands of a very few corporate giants or state actors, forming a trend toward "technological centralization." On the other hand, intelligent technology was once vested with the high hope of "decentralization"—the expectation that it would become an empowerment tool enabling every individual and community to access resources equally, building a flatter, more democratic civilizational form. The collision of these two forces is essentially a contest between centralized technological control and the decentralized ideal of civilization.

Examining real-world cases: The world's top-tier AI computing power and data resources are highly concentrated in a few tech giants like OpenAI (backed by Microsoft), Google, and Meta. Estimates suggest these companies control over 70% of the global high-end AI computing resources. This concentration manifests not only in market monopoly but also in the power to dictate technological development paths and set ethical standards. At the state level, a leading power's export bans on high-end GPU chips aim not only to hinder competitors' industrial development but also to weaponize technological advantage, constructing and maintaining national technological hegemony. This stands in stark contrast to the decentralized ideal of "AI for Good," using technology to solve global challenges like climate change and public health. Viewed through the lens of political philosophy's classic debates, history has repeatedly shown that any absolute power—be it political or technological—unchecked by countervailing forces, carries immense risk. The centralization of intelligent technology gives rise to a new kind of "technological Leviathan":Unlike a government wielding direct violence, it can exercise more secrecy and profound power by controlling information infrastructure, shaping public perception, and determining resource allocation. This directly conflicts with the fundamental imperative in civilizational evolution: "safeguarding freedom through the dispersion and checks and balances of power." The ultimate choice before us is clear: Will technology be used to empower the many, or to consolidate the dominance of the few? This choice will determine whether future civilization trends towards digital feudalism or towards inclusive democracy enabled by technology.

Section 3: Deconstructing the Challenges: Four Core Hurdles in Reconstructing the Intelligent Order

The four great paradoxes are not merely philosophical speculations floating in the air; they are embedding themselves into our reality in an extremely sharp and concrete manner, transforming into a series of "hardcore" challenges demanding solutions. Deconstructing the paradoxes is to better confront the difficulties. The task of this section is precisely to "ground" these four fundamental paradoxes, breaking them down into four core challenges that we must face directly in the realms of law, economics, ethics, and global governance. These challenges are the projections of the paradoxes onto the real world, the concrete roadblocks obstructing the path to an intelligent civilization. They define the most arduous "battlefield" in the current intelligent revolution.

The Data Ownership Challenge: "Who Owns the Data of 'Me'?"

The Data Ownership challenge is the direct landing of the Privacy Paradox and the Power Paradox in the domain of property rights and benefit distribution. Its core question strikes at the very "boundaries of the self" in the intelligent age—when personal life, physiological characteristics, and even behavioral trajectories are transformed into data, who should own the rights and benefits of this "digital double": the source of the data (the user) or the processor of the data (the enterprise)? The answer to this question directly determines the flow of power and profit in the intelligent age.

From a legal perspective, data ownership remains in a grey area. In theory, users are the "producers" of data, but data only generates practical value after being collected, cleaned, labeled, and modeled by enterprises. This split between "production and processing" creates a tug-of-war over property rights definition. The EU's GDPR attempts to strengthen user control through "data subject rights"; its "right to data portability" was originally intended to give users the initiative in data migration, but due to technical format barriers between companies, it has become a difficult-to-implement clause in practice. China's Personal Information Protection Law establishes the "informed-consent" principle, yet the often tens-of-thousands-of-words length of privacy agreements turns user "consent" into a reluctant compromise—most people never truly read the terms but must click "agree" to use the service. This formalistic authorization is, in essence, a passive surrender of user control over data.

More sharp than ownership is the issue of fair distribution of data income rights.When a tech giant relies on the behavioral data of millions of users to train its core AI large model, subsequently gaining hundreds of billions in market capitalization growth and huge profits, the users providing the data "raw materials" receive only "free use of the APP" as compensation, creating an extreme contrast with the immense value created by the data. Although discussions exist around sharing mechanisms like "data cooperatives" and "data dividends",how to quantify the contribution of individual data within an AI model,and how to design distribution rules that balance fairness and efficiency,remain unsolved problems. Conflicts have already emerged in reality:a globally renowned social platform faced massive class-action lawsuits for not informing users that their facial data would be used to train image recognition algorithms;some emerging "data trading platforms" claim to allow users to sell their data,but keep pricing power firmly in the platform's hands, offering users minimal returns,Youdaoplaceholder0 instead intensifies the essence of data exploitation. Youdaoplaceholder1 the core contradiction of this challenge lies in the interest imbalance between "data producers" and "data users"—if a fair framework for ownership and benefit is not established,the loss of the "sphere of self" in the Privacy Paradox will be irreversible,and the technological centralization in the Power Paradox will be increasingly exacerbated by ed by data monopoly.

The Technological Monopoly Challenge: "How to Break the 'Winner-Takes-All' Dynamic?"

The Technological Monopoly challenge is the concentrated eruption of the Employment Paradox and the Power Paradox in market structures and the global landscape. Its essence is how to prevent intelligent technology from being alienated from a "tool for empowerment" into a "new barrier solidifying inequality." In the AI field, the "winner-takes-all" effect far exceeds that of the internet era. This monopoly manifests both in corporate-level market dominance and extends to state-level technological hegemony, creating a dual dilemma.

At the corporate level, giants build almost insurmountable competitive moats by controlling the triple barriers of "Data-Computing Power-Models." Massive user data provides fuel for algorithmic iteration, ultra-large-scale computing clusters form computing power hegemony, and closed-source advanced AI models block the catch-up path for small and medium-sized innovators—these barriers make it difficult for new entrants to establish themselves, even with technical creativity, given the gap in data and computing power. Faced with this reality, traditional antitrust thinking is being tested: Should giants be forced to open their AI model APIs? Should core computing infrastructure be regulated as "critical public facilities"? The US and EU have launched antitrust investigations into some AI giants, but the speed of technological iteration far outpaces the update of regulatory tools. Finding the balance between "not stifling innovation" and "maintaining market fairness" remains an unresolved question.

The dilemma of technological monopoly escalates further at the state level into a game of "technological hegemony." Some technologically leading nations, through high-end GPU export bans, battles for dominance in setting technical standards, and alliance-building initiatives, attempt to weaponize their technological advantage, constructing a "hierarchical order" in the global AI industry chain. This directly leads to the risk of "digital colonization" for developing countries—they struggle to access core technologies and computing resources, remaining trapped at the low end of the industry chain, or even forced into "technological dependency" in building their intelligent infrastructure. In reality,this

Contradiction presents a complex duality: On one hand, a certain AI giant faces joint scrutiny from regulators in multiple countries due to its absolute dominance in the generative AI market; on the other hand, China's practice of transferring smart agricultural technology to African nations to increase crop yield, while seen as a "South-South cooperation" attempt to break technological monopoly, also implies the extension of geopolitical influence. Ultimately, the core conflict of the technological monopoly challenge lies in the imbalance between "incentivizing innovation" and "maintaining fairness and inclusivity"—laissez-faire towards monopoly will exacerbate dominated by giants ance in job markets and the global technological divide, while excessive intervention may stifle the vitality of technological iteration. Furthermore, the divergence between techno-nationalism at the state level and global cooperationism makes resolving this challenge particularly fraught.

The AI Ethics Challenge: "Who Sets the 'Moral Bottom Line' for Intelligence?"

The AI Ethics challenge is the ultimate questioning of the Cognitive Paradox and the Privacy Paradox at the level of value judgment—when AI begins intervention decision-making scenarios concerning human rights and interests, such as medical diagnosis, credit assessment, and judicial sentencing, who should define its "moral code"? And how can we ensure this code aligns with humanity's shared value pursuits? This challenge involves both the technical-level dilemma of "explainability" and civilizational-level conflicts over "value consensus," extending far beyond the purely technical realm.

The core pain point is of technical ethics lies in the "black-box nature" and lack of explainability in AI decision-making. When an AI medical system overrules a treatment plan proposed by a doctor, it cannot provide a logical derivation that convinces both physician and patient; when an algorithmic credit score rejects a user's loan application, the hidden racial or regional biases are difficult to detect—this "result-only, no-reason" decision-making model strips AI ethics of its foundation for accountability, making fairness and justice elusive. A certain AI medical imaging system, due to a lack of samples from a specific demographic in its training data, led to a significantly higher misdiagnosis rate for that group. This case exposed not just a technical flaw, but a lack of ethical review: in technology R&D, developers often focus on "algorithmic accuracy" while neglecting the fairness issues behind "data representativeness." Explainable AI (XAI) is seen as the key to cracking the black box, but current technology still struggles to balance "algorithmic complexity" with "explanation clarity." And even if explainability is achieved, deeper civilizational ethical conflicts will still emerge.

The dilemma of civilizational ethics stems from the diversity of value standards and cultural differences across the globe. Different cultures have inherent variations in defining "privacy," "the right to life," and "fairness": the collectivism in Eastern cultures tends to concede personal privacy moderate for the public good, while the individualism in Western cultures emphasizes the absolute inviolability of privacy; differing religious beliefs about the "beginning of life" also make the ethical boundaries of gene-editing technologies difficult to unify. These differences make the formulation of a "globally unified AI ethics code" extremely difficult—should it be led by Silicon Valley tech elites, Brussels officials, or a multilateral UN forum? This in itself is an ethical controversy full of power games. Leading global AI companies have jointly issued AI ethics initiatives, but on sensitive issues like military AI applications and the use of facial recognition technology, parties diverge greatly due to differing value stances; a global AI ethics committee, when attempting to formulate universal guidelines, reached a stalemate unable to reconcile the views of members from different cultural backgrounds. These realities demonstrate that the essence of the AI Ethics challenge is the shattering of the "myth of technological neutrality"— AI systems, from design to training, are embedded with the cultural backgrounds and value judgments of their designers. Attempting to use purely technical means (like explainable algorithms) to resolve value conflicts is futile.

The Global Governance Challenge: "How to Avoid 'Intelligent Hegemony'?"

The Global Governance challenge is the ultimate manifestation of the Power Paradox and the Employment Paradox in the international political and economic order—the cross-border, supra-sovereign nature of intelligent technology demands a community-based response from humanity, yet the boundaries of national sovereignty and the games of geopolitics plunge global collaborative governance into predicament. This challenge is evident both in the fragmentation of rule coordination and the vacuum in division transnational responsibility, directly impacting the overall direction of human civilization in the intelligent age.

Fragmentation of rule coordination has emerged as a prominent obstacle in global AI governance. Currently, the global AI governance landscape presents a fragmented "multi-track parallel" scenario: The EU adheres to a risk-based "ex-ante regulatory" model, with its EU AI Act imposing strict restrictions on high-risk AI applications (e.g., biometric identification, medical diagnosis) ; the U.S. favors an "ex-post regulation + industry self-regulation" approach, prioritizing innovation dynamism and maintaining a lenient stance toward technological R&D; China adopts an "agile governance" strategy, promoting technology implementation while safeguarding security .Such regulatory differences not only impose heavy compliance costs on multinational enterprises—a multinational autonomous driving company, for instance, must adjust its technical solutions to meet varying national regulatory requirements, leading to the inefficient dilemma of "country-specific strategies"—but also risk triggering bloc-based development of technology. AI systems under different governance frameworks have formed incompatible standards and systems, rendering global collaboration to address common issues such as algorithmic bias and data security empty talk .

More dangerous than rule fragmentation is the "accountability vacuum" for transnational AI incidents. When a Level 5 fully autonomous vehicle, produced by a company from Country A, equipped with an algorithm from Country B, causes a fatal accident in Country C, where does liability lie—with the manufacturer, the algorithm supplier, the owner, or the local government? Existing international law and product liability laws are almost powerless in the face of such "multi-actor, cross-jurisdictional" complex scenarios. An incident involving a social event triggered by an AI recommendation algorithm running on transnational cloud computing services, because the responsible parties involved multiple jurisdictions, ended up in protracted legal disputes, with victims unable to obtain compensation—this accountability vacuum hangs over global governance like a "Sword of Damocles," where a single major incident could detonate a global crisis of trust and economic conflict.

The deepest conflict in the Global Governance challenge lies in the boundary game between "National Sovereignty" and "Global Coordination." In an anarchic international society, every sovereign state finds it difficult to completely cede technological sovereignty and development rights for the sake of global interests; yet the global risks of AI technology (like the cross-border conduction of algorithmic discrimination, the proliferation of autonomous weapons) urgently require a community-based human response. This "tug-of-war between sovereignty and governance" determines whether the future of the intelligent age trends towards confrontation or cooperation—if the limitations of Youdaoplaceholder0 cannot be to build pragmatic global governance mechanisms, the risk of "intelligent hegemony" will persist, ultimately making all of humanity pay the price for technological fragmentation.

These four core challenges do not exist in isolation; they are intertwined and mutually reinforcing: the ambiguity of data ownership provides fertile ground for technological monopoly, which in turn exacerbates the fragmentation of global governance, and the lack of ethical consensus robs all problem-solving of its value anchor. Reconstructing the intelligent order essentially involves finding the balance between technological progress and human values in the process of cracking these challenges—this requires not only innovation in law and institutions but also consensus and cooperation at the civilizational level.

Section 4: Future Prospects: A Multi-layered Action Framework for Human-Led Transformation

The paradoxes and challenges of the intelligent age are not the final chapter of civilization, but existential questions that humanity must collectively answer. Technology itself has no will; the helm determining its direction remains firmly in human hands. This section aims to move beyond critique and deconstruction, building a multi-layered action framework—from the micro individual to the macro global level—that directly responds to the book's core question: How can humanity steer this transformation, rather than be consumed by technology? The answer lies in a shift in identity from passive "adaptor" to active "architect": by fostering individual awakening, corporate responsibility, national regulation, and global coordination, we can re-anchor technology to human values. This is not utopian fantasy, but a proactive choice based on practical pathways, crucial for the survival and flourishing of civilization.

The core task at the individual level is to build "Technological Reflexivity," using this to counter the erosion of subjectivity by the Cognitive and Privacy Paradoxes. In a digital environment where algorithms are omnipresent, defending cognitive autonomy and the dignity of privacy requires accumulating strength through daily actions. Just as managing physical health requires a balanced diet, individuals should consciously construct diversified information intake channels: actively subscribe to high-quality sources that challenge their own views, regularly cleanse algorithmic recommendation feeds that create significant "filter bubble" effects, and even deliberately switch search engines and social platforms to break a single algorithm's monopolistic definition of "reality"— a user interested in current affairs could follow media reports from different stances, piecing together a more complete picture of the world themselves, rather than letting any single information stream shape their cognition. Regarding data authorization, the "minimization principle" must be practiced: refuse a flashlight app access to one's address book, resist a game app's request for real-time location, or, like privacy-conscious users, forego smart door locks that mandate facial recognition in favor of password or card-based alternatives. The essence of these small actions is elevating the individual from a technological "appendage" to a "chooser." Not everyone needs to become a technical expert, only a conscious user—this is the starting point for all change and the first line of defense in guarding the cognitive and privacy boundaries that define "being human."

As the key engine of the intelligent revolution, enterprises must practice a "Human-Centered Technology Philosophy," no longer pursuing efficiency alone, but actively resolving the challenges of technological monopoly and ethics. This requires deeply embedding social value and human well-being into the core of technology R&D and business models, achieving a shift from "what can we do?" to "what should we do?". Similar to risk control processes in finance, enterprises should mandate independent ethical impact assessments before launching every major AI product: establish interdisciplinary ethics committees including philosophers, sociologists, legal experts, and representatives from the general public to review whether algorithms harbor hidden biases, exacerbate social inequity, or excessively capture user attention or data. A leading tech company, before rolling out a new recommendation algorithm, evaluates not only click-through rate improvements but also measures its impact on user mental health and degree of viewpoint polarization, adjusting the model accordingly—a practical application of this concept. Simultaneously, companies need to proactively break down "winner-takes-all" barriers, promoting technological inclusivity and ecosystem co-creation: open basic model APIs to third-party developers and SMEs, providing computing power services at reasonable prices; follow the example of a cloud service giant that proactively deletes redundant user data rather than storing it indefinitely; or emulate a creative AI firm that opens its core image generation capabilities to small design studios, lowering the barrier to using cutting-edge technology. These actions aim to redefine the standards of business success—making "fairness," "inclusion," and "trustworthiness" KPIs as important as "efficiency" and "profit," transforming enterprises from "technology controllers" into responsible "guardians of human value." This is both a strategy for building long-term trust and the only path to sustainable innovation.

As the highest trustee of the public interest, the state needs to establish "Balanced Regulation," building bridges between innovation vitality and social equity to address the Employment Paradox and the Data Ownership challenge. "Balance" means avoiding both the crude stifling of innovation with one-size-fits-all approaches and the laissez-faire neglect of inaction, instead guiding technology towards good through sophisticated institutional design. To counter AI's impact on employment, states must prospectively construct an "AI-Social Safety Net" linkage mechanism: explore levying an "AI Levy"—not on the technology itself, but on enterprises that significantly reduce labor costs through AI adoption, dedicating the revenue specifically to retraining and transitional support for affected workers. The upgraded version of the "flexicurity" model piloted in Nordic countries like Denmark exemplifies this, using state-led, robust vocational training to help workers transition from automated roles to new human-machine collaboration positions. Regarding data rights distribution, the state must move beyond the vague "informed consent" principle, using legislation to clarify that data value is shared by users, enterprises, and society: China's Data Security Law and Personal Information Protection Law have laid the groundwork; the next step could explore "Data Trust" models—where a trustee manages data assets on behalf of users and negotiates profit-sharing with enterprises—or legislate to grant users a right to claim benefits from data derivatives (like AI models trained on their data). The core value of state-level action is upholding social fairness, justice, and worker dignity, transforming the state from a "crisis firefighter" or "technology libertarian" into an "architect of technological order," ensuring the dividends of technology benefit the broader populace and avoiding a digital wealth gap.

The urgent task at the global level is to advance "Coordinated Governance," transcending the old script of geopolitical rivalry to solve the Global Governance and Technological Monopoly challenges. None of AI's challenges are anything but global; no single nation can insulate itself. A "tech cold war" has no winners and would only harm all of humanity. Building a new paradigm of coordinated governance requires abandoning the fantasy of a "world government" and turning instead to pragmatic, multi-layered international mechanisms: establish a "Global Panel on Artificial Intelligence Governance" under the UN framework, similar to the IPCC, composed of scientists, ethicists, legal scholars, and government representatives to provide scientific assessments and policy recommendations based on global consensus; simultaneously, support the WHO in developing global ethical guidelines for AI medical devices, and the ICAO in formulating regulations for autonomous transportation. To narrow the global technology divide, developed nations and tech giants must bear responsibility, avoiding technological colonialism: the World Bank or multilateral institutions could lead the establishment of a "Global AI Development Fund" to finance computing infrastructure and cultivate local AI talent in developing countries; emulate the technology-sharing model of the CGIAR to create a global repository of open-source AI models and data. An international organization providing advanced smart agricultural technology to African farmers at low cost or as open source is a beneficial step in this direction. The ultimate goal of global coordination is to defend the collective interests of the human community, urging nations to transform from "participants in technological confrontation" into "co-builders of a technological civilization"—perhaps the greatest and most arduous collaborative task assigned to humanity in the intelligent age.

The individual's "Technological Reflexivity," the enterprise's "Human-Centered Technology Philosophy," the state's "Balanced Regulation," and global "Coordinated Governance" are not isolated actions but an organic whole, mutually supportive and progressively layered: individual awakening provides the social foundation for corporate and state transformation; corporate transformation provides the market impetus for technology's beneficial application; state regulation builds the institutional framework for global coordination; and global cooperation creates a fair environment for individual and corporate action. The core of this action framework remains "Human-Led Technology"—not rejecting technological progress, but ensuring that every step of its development serves human freedom and comprehensive development. This is the response to all the paradoxes and challenges discussed previously, and the final conclusion of the book's discourse: the ultimate significance of the intelligent revolution lies not in how the technology evolves, but in how humanity, through technology, constructs a new form of civilization that is more dignified, more equitable, and more resilient.

Section 5: The Civilizational Choice: Towards a New Civilizational Form of "Human-Machine Symbiosis"

As the tendrils of intelligent technology reach deep into the nerves of our cities, the fabric of our homes, and even the human body, our discussion has long moved beyond "whether to accept intelligence" to "which intelligent civilization to choose." From the "symbiosis with land" in agricultural civilization to the "collaboration with machines" in industrial civilization, the essence of each human technological revolution has been a redefinition of the "relationship between ourselves and technology." The choice presented by the intelligent revolution is particularly crucial: do we let technology follow the logic of "efficiency first" towards centralization, or do we anchor it to "human values" to build symbiosis? This choice will not only determine the ultimate direction of intelligent technology but also reshape the future form of human civilization. All the discourse in the preceding sections of this chapter—from the passive fate of tools to the proactive environment of intelligence, from the efficiency revolution of the city brain to the equity disputes over data ownership—ultimately points to this civilizational-level proposition. Only by clearly discerning the two possible paths and defining the core connotation of "human-machine symbiosis" can we truly answer the question posed in the introduction, "How should humanity dance with technology?", bringing the book's discourse full circle.

The Clash of Two Civilizational Paths: The Divide Between Techno-Authoritarianism and Human-Machine Symbiosis

The civilizational divide of the intelligent revolution is, in essence, a clash between two value logics. A Techno-Authoritarian Civilization takes "efficiency supremacy" as its core, viewing intelligent technology as an evolutionary force independent of humanity, believing humans need only conform to its resource allocation logic. On this path, data and computing power naturally concentrate in the hands of a few tech giants and technologically leading nations, forming a closed loop of "technological hegemony-resource monopoly-power entrenchment." While ordinary individuals are the source of data, they possess neither ownership nor benefit rights—a tech giant can gain trillions in market capitalization by training AI models on user social data, while users receive only "free use of an APP" as meager compensation; developing countries, due to chip technology barriers, can only rely on computing power exports from developed nations, much like relying on colonial powers for energy supplies in the industrial era. More hidden is the compression of human "room for choice": AI recommendation algorithms filter information based on "optimal efficiency," depriving users of exposure to diverse viewpoints; intelligent employment systems assign jobs based on "skill matching," stripping humans of the right to choose their own careers. Ultimately, this path exacerbates the technological divide and civilizational homogenization—if a healthcare system in an African nation cannot access AI diagnostic algorithms, its public health standards may remain perpetually behind; "family data sharing," valued in Eastern cultures, might be deemed "privacy leakage" by uniform technical standards. Like a species losing genetic diversity, it faces the risk of collapse when encountering technological shocks. Looking back at history, this is merely a reenactment of the "machine enslaves humanity" logic of the industrial revolution, only now the tool has shifted from the steam engine to AI, with penetration reaching human cognition and emotion, making the risks more hidden and harder to reverse.

In contrast, a Human-Machine Symbiotic Civilization takes "Human Value Priority" as its core logic, viewing intelligent technology as a "tool to expand human value," not a rival to replace humanity. On this path, data is a "shared public resource," computing power is "inclusive infrastructure," and technological development consistently balances efficiency and fairness. The EU's GDPR has already established the "right to erasure"; future "data cooperative" models could further enable users to collectively participate in data value distribution; through a "Global Computing Power Sharing Fund," developing countries could access low-cost computing support, akin to the global sharing of electricity resources today. Human "room for choice" would not be compressed but expanded: AI-assisted creative tools could help ordinary people realize artistic dreams without replacing original inspiration; intelligent education systems could customize learning curricula without depriving the right to choose what to learn—just as a painter uses an intelligent brush: the brush

186

outlines precisely, but the painting's emotion and thought are still defined by the painter. In reality, this path is already taking shape: Kenya's M-Pesa smart payment system, adapted to the local "cash-based transaction" culture, allows remote farmers to transfer money without bank accounts, boosting financial inclusion from 26% in 2007 to 83% in 2023; China's "Intelligent Poverty Alleviation System" uses AI to analyze causes of poverty, creating customized assistance plans for each household, helping all 832 impoverished counties escape poverty. These cases prove that human-machine symbiosis is not a fantasy; as long as technology develops around "human needs," a win-win for "efficiency and fairness" is achievable.

The divide between the two paths is an inevitable manifestation of historical law. During the agricultural revolution, the Mesopotamian civilization, with its "land sharing," fostered city-state collaboration, while the Maya civilization, with its "land monopoly," declined due to resource depletion. During the industrial revolution, the "welfare states" of Northern Europe balanced efficiency and fairness, while the "laissez-faire" 19th-century UK plunged into a crisis of wealth disparity. The particularity of the intelligent revolution lies in technology's stronger "self-evolution capability"—AI algorithms can self-learn and optimize, data value grows exponentially with accumulation, and "path dependency" is more pronounced: once the techno-authoritarian logic takes hold, it becomes difficult for individuals and developing nations to reverse the trend; if the human-machine symbiosis logic is implemented, the inclusive nature of technology can form a virtuous cycle. Yet, the current pace of technological development far outstrips the speed of human cognition and governance—ChatGPT's iteration cycle shrank from 6 months to 3 months, brain-computer interfaces moved from lab to clinic in just 5 years. If we do not proactively define the direction of technology, the efficiency logic will naturally lead to authoritarianism; only by actively choosing "human-machine symbiosis" can we ensure technology consistently serves ultimate human goals. This is not the responsibility of any single country or corporation, but a common mission for all humanity, just as tackling climate change requires global coordination; building a human-machine symbiotic civilization also requires the participation of all humankind.

The Core Connotation of Human-Machine Symbiotic Civilization: Technology Expands the Space for Human Value.

The core of "Human-Machine Symbiosis" is a synergistic relationship of "Human-Led Technology, Technology-Empowered Humanity": humans define the value goals of "why to do," technology solves the implementation paths of "how to do," enabling humans to transcend physiological and cognitive limitations and achieve more comprehensive development. This symbiosis does not mean resisting technology, but rather re-anchoring the positioning of "technology and humanity," particularly evident in the three dimensions unique to humans: creativity, empathy, and ethical judgment—these are what intelligent technology can never replace, and they are the ultimate support of human subjectivity.

In the realm of Creativity, technology is the 'brush,' humanity is the 'painter': AI can generate aesthetically pleasing paintings and compose grammatically correct poetry, but it cannot infuse them with the perception of life or the nuanced expression of emotion. Japanese artist Takashi Murakami's Universe Flowers series, created in collaboration with AI, saw the AI generate thousands of drafts, with the final selection and modifications made by Murakami, preserving the AI's precision while retaining a human touch; DeepMind's AlphaFold predicted 200 million protein structures, accelerating drug discovery, but the research direction of "conquering cancer" is still defined by humans—AI is the "pathfinding guide," humanity is the "navigator setting the destination." Without humans, technological exploration loses its meaning.

In the realm of Empathy, technology is the 'bridge,' humanity is the 'conveyor of emotion': AI can assess user anxiety through voice recognition and offer comfort, but it cannot truly feel the physiological discomfort anxiety brings; it can recommend friends with similar interests, but it cannot replace the warmth of face-to-face communication. China's "AI psychological companion system" provides emotional support to left-behind children in remote areas but clearly states, "I am an AI; for real companionship, please contact a community teacher"; smart prosthetics not only help the elderly walk again but also convey the "firmness of a family member's supportive grip" through haptic feedback—technology solves the problem of "insufficient emotional resources," but always preserves the core position of "human emotional interaction." In the social sphere, virtual idols interact with fans via holographic projection, but their management teams still hold offline meet-and-greets to prevent fan dependence on the virtual; smart social platforms use "emotional matching algorithms" to build mutual support communities but employ human moderators to supervise interactions and prevent emotional manipulation—technology makes connection easier, but it cannot make emotions more genuine, and human empathy stems from the "sharing of life experiences," something AI can never simulate.

In the realm of Ethical Judgment, technology is the 'scale,' humanity is the 'rule-maker': AI can calculate the most efficient solution of "sacrificing one to save five," but it cannot judge its conformity with the ethic of "the equal value of life"; it can calculate the option of "prioritizing treatment for the young to save medical resources," but it cannot weigh this against the tradition of "respecting the elderly and caring for the young." In gene editing, AI pinpoints disease-causing genes with precision, but the ethical boundary of "prohibiting germline gene editing" is defined by humans through law; AI-assisted diagnosis improves cancer detection rates, but the choice of "whether to inform the patient" is still made by the doctor based on the patient's psychological state—AI provides "probabilities and ranges," humans make "ethical and value-based" judgments. Human ethical choices stem from a "shared agree of civilizational values"; although different cultures have varying understandings of fairness and justice, the core is always "safeguarding human well-being and civilizational continuity." AI lacks "civilizational agree" and thus cannot replace human ethical decision-making.

Humanity as the Ultimate Arbiter of Civilizational Destiny

Having examined the essence of human-machine symbiosis, we return to the fundamental question posed at this book's inception: How does humanity preserve its agency during this intelligent revolution? How do we learn to dance with technology rather than be consumed by it? The answer reveals itself with clarity: Human agency expresses itself not through rejecting technology, but through proactively shaping our relationship with it. The dance between humanity and technology requires not that we follow technology's logic, but that technology adapts to humanity's value system. The ultimate significance of the intelligent revolution lies not in technology's self-evolution, but in civilization's self-reinvention— through technology, we gain the opportunity to break free from repetitive labor, transcend our physiological and cognitive limitations, and redirect our energies toward domains that embody our essential humanity: creativity, empathy, and ethical judgment. In doing so, we move closer to realizing the comprehensive development of human potential.

The dicourse across the first seven chapters systematically leads to this conclusion. The journey from the "passive nature of tools" to the "proactive environment of intelligence" in Chapter 1 reveals technology's evolutionary trajectory. Chapters 2 through 7, exploring the dimensions of "life," "society," and "cognition," demonstrate technology's transformative impact on human experience. The first four sections of Chapter 8—"reassessing contradictions," "analyzing paradoxes," "deconstructing challenges," and proposing an "action framework"—collectively chart a practical course toward building a human-machine symbiotic civilization. Throughout this exploration, the central theme remains constant: how humanity can steer technological development. Our task is not to resist technological evolution, but to channel it within a framework of human values, ensuring intelligent technology serves as an instrument for expanding human potential rather than becoming the standard by which human worth is measured.

Throughout civilization's long journey, the intelligent revolution represents merely the latest chapter in human evolution. From agricultural civilization using the plow to extend physical capability, to industrial civilization harnessing steam power to amplify energy, to now intelligent civilization employing AI to expand cognitive capacity—humanity has consistently leveraged technology to transcend limitations while never relinquishing its role as technology's guide. The specter of "techno-authoritarianism" we currently face stems fundamentally from a crisis of confidence in our own capabilities. We fear being surpassed by technology, dread losing our agency, yet this anxiety overlooks humanity's defining strength:

our capacity for critical reflection on technology's impact, our ability to correct its course, and our power to collaborate in building a civilizational order aligned with human values.

Ultimately, constructing a human-machine symbiotic civilization requires neither salvation from a "super AI" nor fantasies of a "techno-utopia." It demands only that every individual, organization, and nation remembers this fundamental truth: Technology represents an extension of human civilization, not an independent evolutionary force. Humanity remains the ultimate arbiter of civilizational direction, not technology's passive follower. When we cultivate technological awareness at the individual level, implement human-centered design at the corporate level, establish balanced governance at the national level, and foster coordinated regulation at the global level, the human-machine symbiotic civilization transforms from distant ideal to tangible reality.

The intelligent revolution's ultimate revelation is profoundly simple: However turbulent the technological seas may become, human values remain civilization's steadfast anchor. By holding fast to our pursuit of meaning, our cherishing of emotional connection, and our commitment to justice, we can navigate the age of intelligence while preserving our essential humanity. So long as we remain grounded in what makes us human—the pursuit of meaning, the cherishing of emotion, the commitment to fairness—we will chart a distinctly human course through these technological waters, bequeathing to future generations a world where technology amplifies human potential, and humanity continues to define civilization's course.

Epilogue

We stand at a crease and a crossroads of our era. Intelligent technology has long stepped out of the realm of "future visions" and quietly permeated every fiber of our existence—reshaping our living environments, bodily perceptions, social bonds, and even the underlying logic of our thought. From the instant responses of smart homes to the silent orchestration of city brains; from wearable devices extending human capabilities to algorithms subtly steering cognitive paths: this surging intelligent revolution is less a one-dimensional leap in technology and more a profound restructuring of human civilization.

Yet, the sharpness of technology never equates to human strength. Computing power can expand infinitely, data can accumulate boundlessly, models can iterate endlessly, yet they can never replace the core of "what makes us human"—the capacity for love, the depth of suffering, the meaning in creation, the weight of morality. Precisely when algorithms nudge us toward our "cognitive comfort zones," we must be more vigilant against the inertia of our own thinking; precisely in this moment of increasingly dense virtual connections, we must more fiercely guard the depth and warmth of emotion in real relationships—that "texture of humanity" technology can never replicate.

The intelligent revolution has laid out not a preordained, smooth path, but a field of choices riddled with forks. We can pursue efficiency, but not at the cost of human dignity; we can embrace convenience, but not by surrendering all privacy and autonomy; we can build intelligent systems, but they must serve the well-being of humanity as a whole, not the power and capital of a few. Every choice at each fork defines the boundary of the "technology-human" relationship.

The future is never predetermined. It is written collectively by the choices of every "now." We are both witnesses to this revolution and shapers of its direction. In this historical process of humanity dancing with technology, may we always retain our clarity—that technology is an extension, not a replacement; a tool, not an end; a path, not a destination.

Being human has never been about "what we can create," but

about "why we create, and for whom." Only by anchoring ourselves to human values—compassion, empathy, ethics, freedom, and love— can we truly calibrate civilization's course amid the technological torrent, ensuring the intelligent revolution ultimately becomes a civilizational footnote that "fulfills humanity," not one that "replaces it."

References

1.Arendt, H. (1958). The Human Condition. University of Chicago Press. pp. 25–48.

2.Apple Inc. (2023). Fall detection and emergency SOS on Apple Watch. Apple. https://www.apple.com/watch/features/ n.p.

3.Arnd-Caddigan, M. (2015). Sherry Turkle: Alone together: Why we expect more from technology and less from each other. Journal of Technology Studies, 41(2), 89–91.

4.Bauman, Z. (2000). Liquid Modernity. Polity Press. pp. 51–73.

5.Beck, U. (1986). Risk Society: Towards a new modernity. Sage Publications. pp. 33–56.

6.Baudrillard, J. (1994). Simulacra and Simulation. University of Michigan Press. pp. 17–32.

7.Borgmann, A. (1984). Technology and the Character of Contemporary Life. University of Chicago Press. pp. 89–102.

8.Buber, M. (1970). I and Thou. eBookIt.com. pp. 45–67.

9.Buolamwini, J., & Gebru, T. (2018, January). Gender shades: Intersectional accuracy disparities in commercial gender classification. In Proceedings of the Conference on Fairness, Accountability and Transparency (pp. 77–91). PMLR. pp. 82–88.

10.Cooley, C. H. (2017). Human nature and the social order. Routledge. pp. 62–85.

11.Deleuze, G., & Guattari, F. (1980). A Thousand Plateaus: Capitalism and Schizophrenia (B. Massumi, Trans.). University of Minnesota Press. pp. 3–21.

12.Dennett, D. C. (2013). Intuition Pumps and Other Tools for Thinking. W.W. Norton & Company. pp. 143–158.

13.European Union. (2018). General Data Protection Regulation (GDPR). pp. 12–27.

14.Felten, E. W. (2011). Filter bubbles: What's the problem? Journal of Economic Perspectives, 25(4), 213–224.

15.Foucault, M. (1975). Discipline and Punish: The Birth of the Prison (A. Sheridan, Trans.). Gallimard. pp. 53–78.

16.Foucault, M. (1986). Of other spaces. Diacritics, 16(1), 22–27.

17.Gander, H. H. (2020). Levinas, Emmanuel: Totalité et infini: Essai sur l'extériorité. In Kindlers Literatur Lexikon (KLL) (pp. 1–3). JB Metzler. pp. 1–2.

18.Gibson, D. G., Glass, J. I., Lartigue, C., Noskov, V. N., Chuang, R.-Y., Algire, M. A., Benders, G. A., Montague, M. G., Ma, L., Moodie, M. M., Merryman, C., Vashee, S., Krishnakumar, R., Assad-Garcia, N., Andrews-Pfannkoch, C., Denisova, E. A., Young, L., Qi, Z. Q., Segall-Shapiro, T. H., ... Venter, J. C. (2010). Creation of a bacterial cell controlled by a chemically synthesized genome. Science, 329(5987), 52–56.

19.Giddens, A. (1991). Modernity and Self-Identity: Self and Society in the Late Modern Age. Stanford University Press. pp. 79–94.

20.Giddens, A. (1998). The Consequences of Modernity. Stanford University Press. pp. 41–58.

21.Goffman, E. (2023). The presentation of self in everyday life. In Social Theory Re-Wired (pp. 450–459). Routledge. pp. 452–457.

22.Habermas, J. (1964). The public sphere. In S. Seidman (Ed.), Power and Rationality: Modern society in a critical perspective (pp. 1–24). University of California Press. pp. 5–18.

23.Habermas, J. (1991). The Structural Transformation of the Public Sphere: An Inquiry into a Category of Bourgeois Society (T. Burger, Trans.). MIT Press. pp. 37–52.

24.Habermas, J. (2003). The Future of Human Nature. Polity Press. pp. 29–44.

25.Haraway, D. J. (1988). Situated knowledges: The science question in feminism and the privilege of partial perspective. Feminist Studies, 14(3), 575–599.

26.Heidegger, M. (1954). The question concerning technology. In Vorträge und Aufsätze (pp. 13–44). Neske. pp. 15–32.

27.Heidegger, M. (1962). Being and Time (J. Macquarrie & E. Robinson, Trans.). HarperCollins. pp. 67–89.

28.Heidegger, M. (1971). Poetry, Language, Thought (A. Hofstadter, Trans.). HarperCollins. pp. 41–56.

29.Heidegger, M. (1993). The question concerning technology. In D. F. Krell (Ed.), Basic Writings: From Being and Time (1927) to the Task of Thinking (1964) (pp. 307–341). HarperCollins. pp. 310–328.

30.Ihde, D. (1990). Technology and the Lifeworld: From Garden to Earth. Indiana University Press. pp. 23–41.

31.Illich, I. (1973). Tools for Conviviality. Harper & Row. pp. 59–72.

32.Jonas, H. (1979). Das Prinzip Verantwortung: Versuch einer Ethik für die technologische Zivilisation. Insel Verlag. pp. 37–54.

33.Jonas, H. (1984). The Imperative of Responsibility: In Search of an Ethics for the Technological Age (H. Jonas, Trans.). University of Chicago Press. pp. 49–66.

34. Leakey, L. S. (1961). New finds at Olduvai gorge. Nature, 189(4765), 649–650.

35. Levinas, E. (1961). Totality and Infinity: An Essay on Exteriority (A. Lingis, Trans.). Duquesne University Press. pp. 73–91.

36. Levinas, E. (1961). Totalité et infini: Essai sur l'extériorité. Kluwer Academic Publishers. pp. 68–85.

37. Marcuse, H. (2013). One-Dimensional Man: Studies in the Ideology of Advanced Industrial Society. Routledge. pp. 87–103.

38. Marx, K. (2016). Economic and philosophic manuscripts of 1844. In Social Theory Re-Wired (pp. 152–158). Routledge. pp. 153–156.

39. McLuhan, M. (1964). Understanding Media: The Extensions of Man. MIT Press. pp. 29–45.

40. Mumford, L. (1963). Technics and Civilization. Harcourt, Brace and World. pp. 51–68.

41. Mumford, L. (2010). Technics and Civilization. University of Chicago Press. pp. 47–63.

42. National Institutes of Health (NIH). (2021). CRISPR-based therapies: Current status and future prospects. NIH Genetic Editing Registry. n.p.

43. Neuralink. (2023). Brain-computer interface technology. Neuralink. https://neuralink.com/ n.p.

44. Nature Editorial. (2018). Gene editing and inequality: How to ensure fair access to the next generation of therapies. Nature, 555(7697), 415.

45. Nussbaum, M. C. (2001). Upheavals of Thought: The Intelligence of Emotions. Cambridge University Press. pp. 73–89.

46. Össur. (2023). Proprio smart bionic prosthesis. Össur. https://www.ossur.com/en-us/products/prosthetics/proprio n.p.

47. Owen, T. (2018). The filter bubble: What's the problem? Journal of Economic Perspectives, 25(4), 213–224. pp. 217–222.

48. Pariser, E. (2011). The Filter Bubble: What the Internet Is Hiding from You. Penguin UK. pp. 35–52.

49. Peking University. (2023). Generation Z Digital Content Trust Research Report. Peking University. pp. 18–29.

50. Pieper, J. (1948). Leisure: The Basis of Culture (G. Fitzgerald, Trans.). Ignatius Press. pp. 31–47.

51. Popejoy, A. B., & Fullerton, S. M. (2016). Genomics is failing on diversity. Nature, 538(7624), 161 164. pp. 162–163.

52. Safaricom. (2023). M-Pesa financial inclusion report (2007–2023). Safaricom. https://www.safaricom.co.ke/personal/m-pesa pp. 22–35.

53. Sartre, J.-P. (1944). No Exit (S. Gilbert, Trans.). Vintage Books. pp. 43–56.

54.Searle, J. R. (1980). Minds, brains, and programs. Behavioral and Brain Sciences, 3(3), 417–424.

55.Schweitzer, H. (1923). The Philosophy of Civilization (J. Naish, Trans.). Blackwood & Sons. pp. 89–105.

56.Skinner, B. F. (1953). Science and Human Behavior. Macmillan. pp. 77–92.

57.Supreme People's Court of China. (2022). Provisions on several issues concerning online litigation. Supreme People's Court of China. http://www.court.gov.cn/zixun-xiangqing-351111.html pp. 5–12.

58.Taylor, C. (1989). Sources of the Self: The Making of the Modern Identity. Harvard University Press. pp. 65–82.

59.Turkle, S. (2011). Alone Together: Why We Expect More from Technology and Less from Each Other. Basic Books. pp. 83–101.

60.United Nations. (2006). Convention on the Rights of Persons with Disabilities. United Nations. https://www.un.org/development/desa/disabilities/convention-on-the-rights-of-persons-with-disabilities.html pp. 10–23.

61.Verbeek, P.-P. (2005). What Things Do: Philosophical Reflections on Technology, Agency, and Design. Pennsylvania State University Press. pp. 59–74.

62.Virilio, P. (1977). Speed and Politics: An Essay on Dromology (M. Polizzotti, Trans.). Semiotext(e). pp. 37–52.

63.Xinhua News Agency. (2023). Blockchain-based news verification system. Xinhua News. http://www.xinhuanet.com/ n.p.

64.Zuboff, S. (2019). The Age of Surveillance Capitalism: The Fight for a Human Future at the New Frontier of Power. PublicAffairs. pp. 112–130.

65.Government of the People's Republic of China. (2020). Intelligent Poverty Alleviation System: National Poverty Alleviation Summary Report. http://www.gov.cn/zhengce/2021-02/25/content_5588280.htm pp. 15–28.

66.OpenAI, Google, & Meta. (2023). Global AI computing power concentration report. In Stanford AI Index Report 2023 (pp. 47–62). Stanford University Human-Centered AI Institute. https://hai.stanford.edu/sites/default/files/2023-03/AI_Index_2023.pdf pp. 47–62.

JIN Yang

Author's Introduction:

He is a full-time teacher at the School of Design and Architecture, Zhejiang University of Technology, Hangzhou, Zhejiang Province, China, and serves as a master's degree supervisor.

A member of the China Institute of Architectural Society and the Chinese Society of Landscape Architecture, as well as a council member of the Hangzhou Creative Design Research Association, he also acts as an entrepreneurship mentor at the Zhejiang University of Technology Student Innovation Base and founded the "Chushu" design brand.

A scholar specializing in AI and innovative design, as well as the creation of human settlement spaces, he focuses on AIGC and digital innovation design in teaching. His research encompasses landscape planning and design, landscape aesthetics and spatial form studies, cognitive visual perception and collective wellbeing, along with profound theoretical foundations and practical experience in areas such as historical urban space conservation and revitalization, renovation design of aging spaces, and cultural tourism planning.

www.ingramcontent.com/pod-product-compliance
Lightning Source LLC
Chambersburg PA
CBHW060039030426
42334CB00019B/2402